AMIENS AND MUNICH

COMPARISONS IN APPEASEMENT

by

ERNST L. PRESSEISEN

1978

MARTINUS NIJHOFF

THE HAGUE / BOSTON / LONDON

ISBN 90 247 2067 2

PRINTED IN THE NETHERLANDS

AMIENS AND MUNICH

"Great wonders there are to a sieve," says the beetle in an old Russian story, "so many holes and no way out."

TO

Raymond J. Sontag

Teacher par excellence

TABLE OF CONTENTS

PREFACE

It has not been my intention to write a definitive study of appeasement. Such a work would have to include the French variety, Stalin's appeasement of Hitler between 1939 and 1941, or the appeasement of Japan in 1938 and 1939. I chose the British case for a number of reasons. The opportunity of a comparative model was a challenge, British appeasement was well known, and the structure of the British government remained rather the same in the intervening period between Waterloo and Dunkirk. I admit that Amiens and Munich represent the most dramatic episodes in the story of appeasement, but then the British struggles against Bonaparte and Hitler were of epic proportions.

It was of course unnecessary "to prove" appeasement at Munich, but very few historians had looked at the treaty of Amiens in this way. Much of my research effort was therefore devoted to examining the published material of the earlier period. While I have used some original Addington documents, this work is not primarily an inquiry into unpublished sources but a reinterpretation of well known events that were made public long ago. The flood of publications and revelations of the 1930's continues unabated. I have tried to use the latest studies, especially those that have benefited from the thirty-year rule.

My debts of gratitude extend over a long period since two stints as chairman of the department have delayed this book by at least four years. Financially I have received support from the Council of Deans of Northern Illinois University, the American Philosophical Society, and especially from Temple University. The latter made available two grants-in-aid and study leaves in 1970 and 1975. Without this important encouragement I could not have completed my work. I would also like to thank a number of institutions for their help: the Public Record Office, London; the manuscript division of the British Museum; the Public Record Office in Exeter, Devonshire; the Newberry Library in Chicago; the Library Company in Philadelphia and last but not least the Samuel Paley Library of Temple University. My wife and son have borne the rigors of my scholarship with patience and have become the experts in appeasement.

Philadelphia
August 1976

CHAPTER I

POINT OF DEPARTURE

Whether another study of appeasement can be justified depends largely on the importance of the subject and the approach that is taken. Appeasement is a highly complex phenomenon – subtle, full of crosscurrents and conflicts. It is also a stubborn topic that will not go away, either in historiography or politics. In the political arena it remains a fighting word; witness the statement by the Governor of California, Ronald Reagan, preferring a blood bath to "appeasement of the students."[1] It will not help to call this an isolated incident in politics; the two decades of the Cold War and the fighting in Vietnam were punctuated by charges of appeasement.

The continuing importance of the word "appeasement" in the political world owes much to its imprecision. In the political rough-and-tumble slipshod vocabulary is to be expected, can indeed be quite useful. But why should historical studies indulge in a similar luxury? A later chapter will attempt to define the term. Our first intention is to demonstrate appeasement's importance for historiography by describing the circumstances in which it occurred. As part of this approach the recurrence of appeasement in rather similar periods should add a perspective to our understanding of the subject.

Few will deny that the age of the French revolution and Napoleon, and the Nazi era with its Führer, produced men and movements of revolutionary character. Both periods are usually associated with mass participation in politics and war, as well as the start in one and the perfection in the other of the medias of mass communication. So sharp was the break with previous life styles, both public and private, that those outside the revolutionary circle found it almost impossible to comprehend the turmoil in standards, habits and values. Diplomacy may have suffered more than any other activity in the revolutionary age since tradition occupies so large a part in its procedures.

[1] *The National Observer*, April 13, 1970, p. 6. Recently George Meany called détente with Russia ". . .a policy of appeasement, just plain, ordinary appeasement." *Time*, March 3, 1975, p. 11.

Finally, the "lottery of revolutions" produced its share of "adventurers" (as Pitt said), of which Bonaparte was one and Hitler a later version.

Diplomacy at work in such times and with such men would have to make many accommodations. The English islands, bending under the revolutionary storms, had nevertheless to deal with them, and we find its diplomats in Paris and Berlin working for peace in traditional ways. At least they tried. Yet even the Earl of Malmesbury thought it best to wear the national (tricolor) cockade during his stay in Paris while Sir Nevile Henderson answered the Hitler salute with his "Rule Britannia!"[2] If they had succeeded the diplomatic method would have triumphed over revolutionary dynamism. Since they did not diplomacy was reduced to accommodations which we call appeasement.

The link between appeasement and two revolutionary periods has provided the perspective for appreciating its importance. Our approach to its study disagrees with the efforts of those historians who see appeasement as a constant feature of diplomacy.[3] It may be, but we do not recognize it by that name. Appeasement, as we know it, was practiced during specific periods under revolutionary circumstances and reached its apogee with the treaties of Amiens and Munich. Nor can we accept the statements of Professor Medlicott who prefers to deny it as a policy altogether.[4] To deny the existence of appeasement is to deny the existence of Napoleon and Hitler. But alas, both did exist, and so does our subject.

All along, however, we have proceeded on an assumption: that a clearer understanding of history can be reached by comparing apparently similar periods of history. Comparative history is not foolproof, it certainly will not attract those who insist on the uniqueness of each historical event, but as a method of studying the past it offers exciting possibilities to the open mind that is willing to give it a try.[5]

It is the peculiar character of history that it does not permit the instant recall or replication available to the scientist. We all know that history does not repeat itself, but can parallels in history be as readily dismissed? Obviously, differences will exist side by side with similarities. No two periods are exactly alike and the comparative method does not seek to straightjacket two distinct eras into a wholly confining mold. Nevertheless, once this is admitted

[2] *Diaries and Correspondence of James Harris, First Earl of Malmesbury*, edit. by the third Earl (London, 1845), III, p. 260; Sir Nevile Henderson, *Failure of a Mission* (New York, 1940), p. 41.
[3] Martin Gilbert, *The Roots of Appeasement* (New York, 1966), *passim*.
[4] W. N. Medlicott, *British Foreign Policy Since Versailles, 1919–1963* (London, 1968), xix.
[5] For the best discussion about comparative history, see C. E. Black, *The Dynamics of Modernization, a study in comparative history* (New York: Harper Torchbook, 1966), pp. 35–46.

comparing one age with another, one ideology with another, or one revolution with another remains the nearest method historians have to the
scientific one of repeating experiments in a laboratory. Is it outlandish or
naive to think that a jacobin or a communist may have something in common,
that the appeasement of Napoleon and of Hitler might be similar, or that
England's policies in one revolutionary age could be compared to her policies
in a similarly disturbed but later period?

It would be a simple matter to list the similarities in England's appeasement
of two autocrats. In each age the opponents denounced the agreement as
"peace at any price" or "on any terms," while its supporters announced a
"peace with honor." Both times the peace agreements lasted for a year, the
prime ministers in office served only three years, and the year of peace was
hailed for giving England a pause to gather her strength and unify her people.
Yet such parallels, whether striking or trivial, do not by themselves demonstrate the soundness of this particular study or comparative history in
general. Fortunately, four criteria suggested by Professor Black may aid us in
establishing the validity of comparing the appeasement of different regimes at
different times by the same country.[6]

The first test centers on the "relationship in time." Any research which
seeks to compare events distantly separated in time will find only "nominal
uniformities," while variations increase with the length of the timespan.
Obviously, comparing contemporary events and institutions has the better
chance to be productive, but this should not inhibit attempts to relate episodes
separated in time. A comparative study of appeasement spanning a hundred
and thirty six years does not appear too far apart. The earlier incident took
place at the start of what is usually called "the modern period," the second
example is nearly contemporaneous. It is true that European society changed
enormously in the time between both events, but certain elements such as the
character of the regime appeased, the appeaser, and the revolutionary temper
of each period occur at both ends of the timespan. But these factors belong to
the second category.

The second criterion is crucial: it requires "a careful definition of the
entities being compared." In a direct sense, this means the party being
appeased, the appeaser, and the circumstances of the age in which appeasement takes place. While the First Consul and the Führer may not appear
similar in every respect, the essential character of both regimes was unlimited
power for their executive position. Each had come to power as a result of

---

[6] *Ibid.*, p. 39.

social upheavals in their country amounting to a revolution, and each sustained his power by apparent mass approval and military might. The fact that Bonaparte rode on the flood of a "liberal" revolution and Hitler on a "reactionary" one is a difference to be noted but does not detract from the quintessence of their dictatorship. And in negotiating with these leaders, the *hubris* of this despotic quality had to be taken into account by the English government.

The definition of the appeaser in each period should prove less troublesome. Since the English government in 1802 and 1938 undertook to appease its European enemy, the search for a definition involves the same government at different periods. While in each case a Cabinet government, backed by majorities in Parliament, chose to follow a policy of appeasement, the Addington and Chamberlain governments were not alike. In 1802, Henry Addington sat in an unreformed House of Comons; in 1938, Neville Chamberlain had to answer to a democratically elected House. Had the domestic forces which shaped foreign policy been democratized, however? Had concern for the Empire, for the preservation of English society, or for the cost of war lost support as determining factors in British foreign policy? Were those influencing foreign policy in 1938 so different from the circles who determined it in 1802? Despite her great electoral reforms some basic qualities in English life had not altered much over a hundred and thirty six years.

The age of the French revolution and the Nazi era furnished the stage for the acts of appeasement. At first glance these periods do not have much in common. The French revolution occurred in an aristocratic century, its program presented a reasoned appeal for the rights of man, and it attracted a largely middle class following. But this ideal picture did not correspond with the realities as seen from London, where French imperialism and jacobin ideology were regarded as the twin disturbers of the age. The social conservatism of the British islands survived the assault of French egalitarianism; in contrast with Europe it offered an alternative which was accepted as a challenge in Paris.

The circumstances of the Nazi revolution are far more complex. It must be understood against a background of the first world war, defeat, and frustrated nationalism. The upheavals in Russia should also be added to this account. If Nazi ideology had little appeal (unlike communism), Nazi imperialism disturbed the fragile peace. Eventually Hitler's assault on the European balance of power proved as dangerous as any effort of Napoleon. Admittedly, the definition of both revolutions demonstrates their differences. The Nazi revolution was "reactionary" and had a limited attraction; the French revolution was universal in its "progressive" or "liberal" character.

Nazi ideology was racist and directed primarily at Germans, but the ideological picture is complicated by the simultaneous strength of communism. In fact, nazism and communism should be compared as a single ideological factor with jacobinism in order to appreciate the revolutionary character of both periods.

The third category in testing the viability of comparative appeasement concerns "the use of evidence." This is not a subject which can make use of quantitative data; the thoughts, passions and calculations which go into the formulation of a policy are not reducible to statistics. Though the words of men may lead to widely differing interpretations, if taken together with their actions one can arrive at an understanding of their policies. This is no easy matter and large amounts of printed or manuscript materials must be synthesized. We are speaking, then, of a fairly traditional method of historical research involving the compilation of data by reading and analyzing all available materials pertinent to the subject. In doing so the author must constantly ask himself three questions: is this or that item of consequence for my topic; am I seeing all the implications of my subject; am I omitting or discarding data which could detract from the validity of my hypothesis?

The last question is especially significant and will be discussed further on in this chapter. The conventional historical method can be enhanced in two ways: by the selection of an imaginative subject for study and through the widest possible use of sources. Even so, rigorous honesty in the use of the evidence will not be enough. A certain measure of doubt must supplement the tentative conclusions, exceptions must be admitted, and general conclusions will possess more credibility if it is allowed that these do not apply in all cases. In short, conclusions based on historical evidence remain a series of approximations.

A fourth test to measure the limits of comparative history concentrates on the formulation of generalizations. For those who eschew generalizations comparative history can have no attractions. Granted its many pitfalls, the comparative method offers the best chance to go beyond history as mere chronology and to arrive at those comprehensive conclusions that evidence plus insight allows. In the case of appeasement this approach presents unique opportunities. A simple retracing of appeasement's march, beyond establishing every detail, can contribute little to understanding the causes, motives or structure of this policy. A comparative study, however, has the fair chance to answer such questions and obtain the perspective that is granted with time. It may be able to decide under what circumstances appeasement is likely to occur, whether it is a desirable policy, and what is has achieved in previous attempts.

The cause of comparative history and the search for appeasement both would be poorly served if this study did not select its models carefully. It is wiser to choose fewer examples which conform closely to the "perfect model" than to range widely and render a comparative project null. To design a comparative study of appeasement which might be successful should not be confused with a prearranged selection of data which forecloses objective conclusions. The latter is not our intention.

The choice of the treaty of Amiens and the appeasement of Napoleon will stand the test of comparison with the pact of Munich and the appeasement of Hitler. It was chosen exactly for this reason: in 1802 and in 1938 Great Britain freely conceded to the demands of a continental autocrat. It had not done the same for Louis XIV or Wilhelm II. Why? One answer has already been suggested. Bonaparte and Hitler were the embodiment of revolutionary storms which the English did not fully understand and could not overcome. Other factors, which are part and parcel of the domestic history of Great Britain, contributed their share. These will form the core of our work.

Can Hitler and Napoleon be so readily equated? In many respects they are of course not the same, but where the European continent was concerned their visions were remarkably alike. The conqueror's road to European unity was each time blocked by the English government and in their relations with England Napoleon and Hitler went through nearly similar experiences. This is a crucial factor in our historical analogy. The treaty of Amiens concluded peace after eight years of war but the Munich pact was a diplomatic agreement to keep the peace. How can these be compared? True, but the difference is more apparent than real. The treaty of Amiens followed immediately upon the conclusion of the war, during which there were at least four separate negotiations to make peace. The pact of Munich came after four years of war and twenty years of sparring between England and Germany which saw many attempts to establish more peaceful relations. In short, agreement came after a long period of conflict in both cases.

The singular position of Great Britain before the Amiens and Munich pacts also justifies their choice as models to compare appeasement. Despite alliances, coalitions, subsidies, or military staff talks, when the diplomatic chips were down Great Britain stood alone. At times the soul of resistance, in 1801 and 1938 she found little support among the rest of Europe. For an island this isolation was acceptable and at times she found it a refuge militarily and psychologically. "I was abandoned by everybody, Allies and *all*," declared George III to the Earl of Malmesbury. Again in 1939, "N[eville] C[hamberlain] seemed... rather angry with all foreigners – Hitler and the Bolshies for their duplicity, the French for giving confidential information away."[7] With this attitude caution seemed the better part of valor and the English government adjusted its policies accordingly. In Europe this meant the abandonment of the balance of power, and Prime Ministers Henry Addington and Neville Chamberlain chose to do so whether they realized it or not.

Caution had, however, its domestic side as well. Our comparative search for the meaning of appeasement should reaffirm the domestic origins of foreign policy. The popular acclaim for Bonaparte's emissary, bringing the ratification of the peace preliminaries to London in October, 1801, fully equalled the popular enthusiasm for Neville Chamberlain returning from Munich in September, 1938. The ecstasy for peace contributed a major share to both agreements. Nor was it a sudden effervescence. The pressure for peace had been increasing for a long time and among many segments of English society, each of which had its own reasons for avoiding or ending foreign conflict. Just as peace came suddenly it seemed to vanish in a year over a trifle. War for Malta in 1803 matched war over Poland in 1939. Yet Switzerland (or Holland) in 1802 and Czechoslovakia in 1938 had been worth the sacrifice to secure peace.

Many sources can participate in the development of a foreign policy but its execution is usually restricted to a very small group. In either case the problem of motive should figure very large in an analysis such as ours. But what is motive anyway? Is it what men say, what they do, or what they *believe* to be true? The latter state is frequently the most important. Pitt (and Addington) apparently believed in 1801 that Bonaparte had "become more moderate." Neville Chamberlain concluded there was "a side of Hitler that would surprise many people."[8] Even these fleeting expressions show a motive, though it would be more realistic to assume that the policies of England's ministers were based on careful calculation and weighing of the odds.

In any event, the search for motive is the search for the wellsprings of appeasement. Such an inquiry must take account of the influences preying on man's mind, the circumstances of the times, and the persistence of historical memories. If it is done on a comparative basis, and the recurrence of events and consequent decisions becomes clear, it will surely provide some general principles and conclusions about appeasement. We can expect no more.

It might be appropriate to close this chapter with a few words about the conscientious use of historical sources. Supposedly every generation rein-

---

[7] Malmesbury Diaries, *op. cit.*, IV, p. 65; John E. Wrench, *Geoffrey Dawson and Our Times* (London, 1955), pp. 394–395.

[8] Malmesbury Diaries, *op. cit.*, IV, p. 67; Keith Feiling, *The Life of Neville Chamberlain* (London, 1946), pp. 363–364.

terprets history in the light of its own experience. Consequently, it is fair to say that very few historians have examined appeasement on a comparative basis or have discussed the treaty of Amiens from this standpoint. Most of the sources for this study were published materials which provided endless details on the English struggles with their European enemies, the patriotic response, the drum and trumpet variety of history. There was defiant oratory in Parliament and heroic activity in battle. But there were other events as well, less publicized in print, concerning civil unrest, food rioting, negotiations for peace, or attempts to buy peace through bribery.

The historian testing a new interpretation relative to appeasement will encounter no problems of "proving" its existence at Munich but faces this obstacle at Amiens. Has he arrived with preconceived ideas, has he ignored the mountains of loyalty in order to find the molehill of dissent? In short, has he, in order to discover appeasement at an earlier period, ignored the majority of history in favor of a few isolated events?

The problem is hardly new and yet has to be faced with each fresh excursion into the past. It requires a wrestling with the sources, with those inconvenient facts that do not "fit," and ultimately with one's private judgment. Whether this effort can be productive depends on the formulation of the topic. If the project breaks new ground, if it strives to gain new insight from old sources through an imaginative hypothesis, the historian should repair the balance between the obvious and the less evident parts of the past. For each belongs to history.

CHAPTER II

APPEASEMENT DEFINED

The face of appeasement has many lines. There are numerous profiles of this face but few images have given a multidimensional representation. It is not hard to understand why this should be so. Few words have changed in a brief span, as appeasement has, its meaning from a positive sense to a negative, indeed pejorative tone.

Appeasement is an old word. According to *The Oxford English Dictionary* is was already in use by the fourteenth or fifteenth century. It defines the term as "the action or process of ... pacification, satisfaction." This source also gives several definitions of the verb "appease," one of which suggests "to pacify, by satisfying demands."[1]

To bring peace, to create calm, to satisfy demands of persons or institutions: all these are part of the meaning of the word "appeasement." Similarly, these conditions form a major portion of the practice of diplomacy. In this general sense, then, appeasement has always been a constituent of diplomacy. We need not go so far as A. J. P. Taylor who has chosen to call "appeasement ... the noblest word in the diplomatic vocabulary."[2] But the need to allay fears, suspicions, ill-humor or ill intentions has inclined the diplomat to appease (i.e. to pacify) his antagonists. This appeasement might be achieved through charm, flattery, humor or bribery, to mention but a few methods. Bribery on this level is of long standing, and if not respectable it is certainly acceptable as a diplomatic method.

Let us be clear about this discussion. We are describing traditional diplomatic habits. Bribery as a type of appeasement called for limited concessions; the worst it might involve was the expenditure of large amounts of money.

---

[1] *The Oxford English Dictionary*, Volume I (Oxford, 1933), pp. 399–400. These pages cite many examples how both verb and noun were used in the past. E.g. in 1430, *Instructions for ambassadors* spoke of "the' Appesement of these Werres," while in 1579 appears the phrase "for appeasement of their ancient controuersies."

[2] A. J. P. Taylor, *The Trouble Makers; Dissent over Foreign Policy, 1792–1939* (Bloomington, Ind., 1958), p. 18.

Moreover, this procedure was expected to obtain results fairly soon and therefore, if undertaken, had a reasonable anticipation of success. There was no reason in the world to name this activity appeasement (Bismarck called it *schmieren*); though the term very occasionally appears it was neither a specific system nor a policy.

Insofar as concessions were a part of diplomatic negotiations, they were closely tied to *quid pro quo*, the balance of power, and a careful calculation of position and advantage. Peace conferences following successful wars could disregard some of these limitations since the victorious powers dictated terms. But peace treaties did not represent regular diplomatic activity; instead, they ratified the use of force. Force, or the threat to use force, did not enter the diplomatic routine and concessions, when made, were the result of calculations, not threats. Ideological factors – what Edmund Burke called "armed doctrine" – were also outside the realm of diplomatic concerns; at the least, the professional diplomat discounted their influence, or he did not know how to deal with them.

In the twentieth century the term appeasement began to be used more frequently in reference to diplomatic activity. Especially where Germany was concerned one encounters the word from the time of World War I, and with the 1920's English writers and statesmen used it freely. "We regard Locarno, not as the end of the work of appeasement and reconciliation, but as its beginning . . ." declared Sir Austen Chamberlain in the House of Commons.[3] The British Foreign Secretary was using the expression in its traditional sense and simultaneously linked it with reconciliation. This appeasement meant to conciliate a Germany estranged from the European community of states, but it was richer in words than in deeds. Yet this is no surprise. The Weimar republic lacked power and prestige; successive British governments treated it barely with respect.

Recently some historians have further confused the issue by defining Locarno as the first appeasement of Germany.[4] As an international agreement Locarno amounted to a mutual hands-off policy. Germany was weak, and after the occupation of the Ruhr sought protection against further encroachments. The treaty relaxed tensions throughout Europe, and the concessions granted Germany were intended to restore the balance between her and France. The Weimar republic was in no position to pressure or to threaten the other signatories to make such concessions. British foreign policy

[3] As quoted in Martin Gilbert, *The Roots of Appeasement* (New York, 1966), p. 115.
[4] Gordon Wright and Arthur Mejia, Jr., *An Age of Controversy* (New York, 1965), pp. 178–179.

hoped to conciliate the German government, but its aim and attitude does not compare to the appeasement of Bonaparte or Hitler. Sir Austen Chamberlain voiced only some polite sentiments about a distinctly unequal state.

We have quoted *The Oxford English Dictionary* (1933 edition) to obtain the earlier definition of appeasement. In its association with traditional diplomacy the meaning of the term changed after 1933 almost as much as diplomacy itself. By 1967 *The Random House Dictionary of the English Language* (unabridged edition) found that "to appease is to make anxious overtures and often undue concessions to satisfy the demands of someone with a greed for power, territory, etc." Obviously, this definition fits the Munich pact, or for that matter the Amiens treaty, much better than the Locarno agreements. The two definitions, separated by thirty years, highlight the change in meaning but do not help in our understanding of the word. A satisfactory conceptualization of appeasement can only be attained by examining its structure and defining it as a policy. It is essential for the comparative approach that we explain our terms.

There have of course been previous attempts to treat the phenomenon of appeasement. It would be futile to detail these here, especially since not a few have preferred justification or condemnation to explanation. Yet two or three arguments cannot be ignored, not because they said so much but rather who presented them. The first are the comments of Sir Orme Sargent, a senior official of the British Foreign Office in the 1930's. In a private letter to J. W. Wheeler-Bennett (who had just completed his book on Munich) he wrote at some length about the nature of appeasement.[5] According to Sir Orme

It becomes questionable as a method of negotiation only if it can be shown to be *immoral*; i.e. the appeaser sacrifices the rights and interests of a third party and not his own when making his concession; or if it is clearly *dangerous*, i.e. where the concession made seriously undermines the strength of the appeaser . . . and lastly when the whole process of appeasement is just ineffective . . .[6]

The question of effectiveness concerned him greatly. If appeasement promised rescue from a truly critical situation, the method ought not to be rejected solely because "it savoured of sharp practice (necessity knows no law) . . ." But when concessions had to be repeated, appeasement became "nothing less than blackmail." In that case its ineffectiveness must condemn it. Sir Orme, a good English pragmatist, drew the conclusion that the humiliation of appeasing Hitler should have been avoided.

[5] J. W. Wheeler-Bennett, *Munich: Prologue to Tragedy* (New York, 1948); the letter is to be found in Appendix 5 of Gilbert, *Roots of Appeasement*, pp. 220–223.

[6] Gilbert, *op. cit.*, p. 220.

...we knew he could not be appeased, and mark you it was humiliation, not because it was immoral, not because it was dangerous, but solely because it was ineffective, useless and a sham.[7]

A high civil servant closely associated with these events can be expected to show such wisdom afterwards. But he was not alone. After the war others tried to account for appeasement. Among them Sir Winston Churchill can hardly be regarded as one of its apologists. In 1950, speaking in the House of Commons, Sir Winston declared:

Appeasement in itself may be good or bad according to the circumstances. Appeasement from weakness and fear is alike futile and fatal. Appeasement from strength is magnanimous and noble, and might be the surest and perhaps the only path to world peace.[8]

Was he thinking of Locarno when he made these remarks? We don't know. The tendency to distinguish one type of appeasement from another is not unusual, however.

In the past twenty years various scholars have tried to differentiate between appeasement and what Hans Morgenthau has called "a corrupted policy of compromise." One of these efforts went beyond the usual superficialities. In 1963 George Lanyi discussed "the problem of appeasement" in an article.[9] For him there were two kinds: active and passive appeasement.

The passive type takes place

...when a power permits its potentially or actually aggressive adversary to improve its position considerably by violating peace treaties, by accumulating massive armaments, and by developing economic and ideological spheres of interests.[10]

Clearly, the label of passivity stems from the lack of response. Aside from a possible moral condemnation, or an appeal to world public opinion, the appeasing state does nothing to stop its enemy. Its vital interests may be threatened in the particular area where its opponent seeks to expand, but it hesitates to improve its own defenses. Passive appeasement "tends to underrate both the increasing strength and the aggressive intention of its adversary."

Active appeasement does not show such hesitations. When faced with "certain concrete demands or grievances" by an aggressive or expansionist

---

[7] *Ibid.*, p. 222.
[8] As quoted in Gilbert, *Roots of Appeasement*, p. ix.
[9] George A. Lanyi, "The Problem of Appeasement," *World Politics*, XV (January, 1963), pp. 316–328. The quote of Hans Morgenthau is from p. 318.
[10] *Ibid.*, p. 319.

power, the latter could expect a sympathetic hearing from the appeasers. In fact the potential aggressor got much more. The negotiations which were begun eventually conceded "all or most of the demands." Moral factors may enter these discussions but are not necessarily an important part. Mr. Lanyi admits that active appeasement cannot be very sharply delineated from the passive variety, and that the practice (be it active or passive) "may . . . invite irreconcilable demands, or even a war of aggression."[11]

Although his analysis does not probe its structure in depth, Lanyi's efforts represent an advance from previous attempts that distinguish only between "good" (i.e. traditional) and "bad" (i.e. recent) appeasement. A part of this shortcoming is his one-dimensional approach: he failed to consider any earlier forms of appeasement and based his discussion solely on the Munich case.

The amoebic quality of our subject does not make understanding it any easier. To obtain a construct of it – i.e., to conceptualize appeasement – will require determining all its characteristics and particulars. No other method seems adequate for our study.[12]

What appears so striking about appeasement is first of all its lack of planning. Perhaps it would be better to call it a lack of foresight, since plans existed to negotiate a peace with France and a *détente* with Germany. Chamberlain wanted closer relations with Germany and had apparently laid down a series of steps to bring this about. Yet what happened in 1938 bore no relation to his plans. In fact, appeasement policies are almost always panic or impulse policies with visions that are very limited.[13] The objective (peace) to be reached is so important that not much thought is given to events or policies in the following period. It is then that the lack of foresight becomes most apparent, and the implications of appeasement lead to disastrous results. As an illustration one can cite the almost identical sequel to Amiens and Munich. Both Napoleon and Hitler told England that the affairs of Europe were no longer her concern.[14]

Appeasement is similarly ill-equipped to deal with the balance of power. It seems strange that Great Britain, an island otherwise so sensitive to coalitions

---

[11] *Loc. cit.*

[12] The question of motives for appeasement, interesting but quite separate from this discussion, will be treated in another chapter.

[13] See e.g. the comments of H. R. Trevor-Roper, "The dilemma of Munich is still with us," *The New York Times Magazine*, (September 15, 1968), p. 84.

[14] For Napoleon's attitude, see A. W. Ward and G. P. Gooch, ed., *The Cambridge History of British Foreign Policy, 1783–1919*, Vol. I, 1783–1815 (Cambridge, 1939), p. 310, and Harold C. Deutsch, *The Genesis of Napoleonic Imperialism* (Cambridge, Mass., 1938), p. 92; Hitler's views are cited in Henri Noguères, *Munich, "Peace for Our Time"* (New York, 1965), pp. 349–350.

on the continent, would twice pursue policies which involved serious misconceptions about the balance of power. When the definitive treaty of Amiens
was being debated in the House of Commons, William Windham, secretary at
war in the first Pitt cabinet, charged that "the whole continent of Europe is
abandoned to France."[15] He was indeed close to the truth. A few months
later, Henry Addington wanted to aid the Swiss in their struggles with
Bonaparte. He soon discovered that his earlier appeasement had upset the
balance of power and that England could do nothing for the Swiss republic.
In a similar vein, Arnold Toynbee has written that "Chamberlain was not
thinking of Anglo-German relations in terms of the Balance of Power at all
. . ."[16]

World War I and Wilsonian idealism had made power politics and the
concept of the balance of power very unpopular in Great Britain. Those who
still advocated its principles were denounced as warmongers.[17] A comparable revulsion against force as a policy had occurred in the war with France,
especially after 1800. The miscalculations which followed were not only the
consequence of errors in judgment, though appeasement was rich in these too.
Rather, appeasement preferred to forget or ignore the balance of power
altogether, hoping perhaps to put a better "system" in its place. Since
appeasement is makeshift, and the balance of power is not, the two could only
interact in a negative sense. The balance of power would be upset by
appeasement's mistakes, but the subsequent disturbances destroyed the credibility of appeasement as a policy. Furthermore, rejection of the balance of
power was only the most obvious of appeasement's miscalculations. Similar
errors were made in assessing the relative (to Britain) military strength of
France in 1801 or Germany in 1938.

Confrontation may be called the third element of appeasement. It is a
circumstance closely tied to our subject, because appeasement seems forever
to take place under the duress of confrontation. This confrontation may
involve different systems of ideology and government, powers varying in size,
or even a clash of personalities. But regardless of such details, confrontation
includes the potential of force as a sequel. Its possibility makes the careful
planning and execution of policies very difficult if not impossible, and, what is
worse, hurried calculations and decisions lead to mistakes that have been
described already as panic policies. In short, appeasement invariably operates

---

[15] [William Cobbett, ed.], *The Parliamentary History of England from the Earliest Period to
the Year 1803* (London, 1820), XXXVI, p. 742.

[16] Dwight E. Lee, *Munich, Plot or Tragic Necessity?* (Lexington, 1970), p. 68.

[17] See the excellent discussion in Keith Robbins, *Munich, 1938* (London, 1968), especially pp.
123–133.

under the gun. Chamberlain flew three times to Germany in order to avoid
war in Central Europe; Addington and his Foreign Secretary, Lord Hawkesbury, prepared for an invasion of England in 1801.[18] Confrontation does not
inhibit negotiations but seems to increase their tempo.

Appeasement would mean little without concessions. Yet as another side of
our definition its purpose remains unclear. This uncertainty touches the
practice of concessions itself as much as the extent of it: in other words, are
concessions to be condemned outright, or only the excessive use of them?
What are concessions supposed to accomplish: to buy time for the appeaser,
or to inaugurate a new era of improved relations? Addington fully matches
Chamberlain in extravagant hopes. Long before "peace for our time," Addington celebrated the preliminaries of peace with France with the words:
"This is not an ordinary Peace: it is a reconciliation between the two first
Nations of the world!"[19] When such dreams evaporate concessions are
presented in a different light. Great Britain needed peace, she could not enter
(or continue) a struggle unprepared and lacked unity at home. In short, she
needed a breathing space. Pitt said it, the partisans of Chamberlain repeated
it, and it remains one of the stock arguments in defending concessions to
Napoleon or Hitler.[20]

Have we exhausted the list of explanations? Hardly. Concessions can be
viewed in still a different light and which is perhaps the most interesting. In
making concessions the appeaser sought neither time nor better relations, but
tried to "satiate" his opponent. The "burden of property" would at one and
the same time make the enemy more cautious and responsible. The fear to lose
in war what had been gained by diplomacy would moderate his conduct from
now on. Lord Castlereagh was of the opinion that "from the moment France
has acquired colonial and maritime resources, she will have more reason to
apprehend the recurrence of hostilities, and will from that moment have more
just and serious causes to refrain from war."[21] Even the twentieth century did
not go that far, though Lord Allen of Hurtwood told a circle of friends at All

---

[18] Henry Addington complained to his brother Hiley that the newspapers were "too tame on
the subject of Invasion." Henry Addington letter to Hiley Addington, August 29, 1801, "Addington Papers," 1801 box, Devon Record Office, Exeter. On July 21, 1801, the Horse Guards had
issued a warning that invasion was imminent. *Letters of Admiral of the Fleet, The Earl of St.
Vincent*, ed. by David B. Smith, (London, 1922), I, pp. 121–122; Philip Ziegler, *A Life of Henry
Addington, First Viscount Sidmouth* (New York, 1965), pp. 121–122.

[19] *Letters of . . . the Earl of St. Vincent*, I, p. 283.

[20] For Pitt's statement, see *Diaries and Correspondence of James Harris, First Earl of Malmesbury* (London, 1845), IV, pp. 67–68; Keith Feiling, *The Life of Neville Chamberlain* (London,
1946), p. 359.

[21] As quoted in George Pellew, *The Life and Correspondence of the Right Honorable Henry
Addington, First Viscount Sidmouth* (London, 1847), II, p. 44 footnote.

Souls' that he "would let Hitler have whatever he wants in Eastern Europe."[22]

While the uncertainty about the purpose of concessions remains, one thing is very clear: appeasement thrives on conceding other people's property. There has never been much doubt in the appeaser's mind that territory other than his own is quite suitable for making concessions. This dubious practice, whether in Dutch colonies or Czech borderlands, emphasizes the questionable character of concessions as a part of appeasement.

(5) A complete account of appeasement must also recognize that its effect is not irrevocable. To be sure, the risks inherent in the policy are great, but appeasement has always stopped short of the point of no return. No matter how far Great Britain pursued her efforts in appeasement, she maintained a core of self-reliance and protection from which a change in policy could be initiated. Canning might huzza that "the British fleet has not been burned," but poetic license aside, did England yield any of her own territory (not counting that recently conquered) at Amiens or Munich? None! Her power and influence was adversely affected by these settlements but her empire was unimpaired, her fleet intact and her shores untouched. Appeasement granted much, often too much – witness leaving the Netherlands and Belgium in French hands in 1802 – but it did not end the appeaser's chance for maneuver or change in attitude and policy. England's independence was preserved.

There is in appeasement the additional tendency toward false economy, or an inclination to conclude bad bargains. At times, instead of war, it can be argued that it is cheaper to appease. The thought of buying peace occurred long before our own time. In March, 1803, the British Ambassador in Paris, Lord Whitworth, faced the prospect of renewed fighting between England and France. While the issue between them concerned the evacuation of Malta, Whitworth proposed to bribe those around Bonaparte as much as two million pounds sterling. Considering what one month of war would cost, it would be "oeconomy" to spend this sum to avoid hostilities.[23] Nothing came of it in the end since Malta was not evacuated and war followed.

The effort to buy an agreement "on the cheap" is typical of appeasement, and in the twentieth century might be interpreted as a businessman's solution

---

[22] Martin Gilbert and Richard Gott, *The Appeasers* (Boston, 1963), p. 35. Leopold Amery had supposedly said the same thing when he told the Germans: "You can't have colonies, but Eastern Europe lies before you." As quoted in Margaret George, *The Warped Vision: British Foreign Policy, 1933–1939* (Pittsburgh, 1965), p. 218.

[23] The British Museum, Manuscript Room, "Liverpool Papers," Add. mss 38238, Vol. 49, Lord Whitworth (Paris) to Lord Hawkesbury, March 24, 1803-most secret and confidential, in cipher. See also Carl Ludwig Lokke, "Secret Negotiations to maintain the Peace of Amiens," *American Historical Review*, XLIX (October, 1943–July, 1944), pp. 55–64.

for international conflicts. The argument is simple enough. War, and the preparations for war, are expensive policies which no government can pursue with a light heart. A nation exhausted by a long struggle (England in 1801), or drained by a world war and a depression would look for alternatives to more military spending. Under the circumstances, a "deal" to avoid the consequences of a war policy seemed very logical, yet invariably appeasement proved to be a bad bargain. Why? Those seeking an agreement miscalculated the relative position of the bargainers and misjudged the mentality of their opponents. Besides, "it is hard to convince the trader that those he meets in the market are not there to buy and sell but to burn down the emporium and build a gladiatorial school."[24]

One of the most striking aspects of appeasement is its penchant to live on illusion and myth. In a certain sense history consists of what people *believe* to be true, but appeasement developed this tendency into a habit. The result was a policy woven of hopes, miscalculations, poor judgments and fear. "Most appeasers were almost unbelievably deficient in their analysis of human nature...," and this conclusion of George Lanyi holds true as much for Bonaparte as for Hitler.[25] It is not that they were alike but that the English responses to them as historical phenomena were so similar. It was a mixture of hope and optimism about human nature, in one sense rather English, i.e. insular, and because Pitt and Addington, Chamberlain and Lord Lothian (to name just a few) proceeded at least in part not on what was, but on what they *believed* to be.

This misreading of Napoleon's or Hitler's character extended to the nature of the regimes as well, and accounts for the myth that careful concessions might dampen its expansionist zeal. Nothing in the English system of government had prepared its leaders to grasp the realities of revolutionary France or Nazi Germany. Though Addington and Chamberlain were warned about the ferocity of their opponents, each chose to disregard such information, to disbelieve his informants, and to continue to hope in the reasonableness and potential moderation of these tyrants.[26] The end of appeasement can be

---

[24] F. S. Northedge, *The Troubled Giant: Britain among the Great Powers, 1916–1939* (New York, 1966), p. 621.

[25] Lanyi, "The Problem of Appeasement," p. 321.

[26] One contemporary expression of these hopes can be found in Robert Bisset, *The History of the Reign of George III to the termination of the late war* (London, 1803), VI, pp. 438–439. Addington voiced his hopes that "the Peace wd. be permanent" to the American minister, Rufus King. *The Life and Correspondence of Rufus King*, ed., by Charles R. King (New York, 1897), IV, pp. 8–9 "Note of a conversation on November 2, 1801 between R. King and Mr. Addington." Addington's evaluation of Bonaparte is in Pellew, *op. cit.*, II, p. 54. For England's illusions during the 1930's, and Chamberlain's in particular, see Christopher Thorne, *The Approach of*

traced from the moment when these illusions were shattered, when policies based on false hopes had lost all credibility. Chamberlain may have been reluctant to face realities, Addington was forced to do so by Napoleon's aggressive policies. And if without myth appeasement could not survive, neither could its most prominent spokesmen.

No one could describe appeasement in measured steps; in its final stages it gives much more the impression of being precipitous. Diplomatic negotiations may take months, even years, yet the harvest of appeasement can be collected in weeks or days. Pitt negotiated for five years with the French republic in the search for peace, yet Addington rushed into an agreement six months after attaining office. Similarly, Stanley Baldwin fumbled for years towards an understanding with Germany without ever quite reaching it, or perhaps wanting to. But Neville Chamberlain felt no constraints (or doubts) about an agreement with Hitler, and reached the summit of appeasement sixteen months after becoming Prime Minister. The difference in time would not be significant but for the issues which had restrained Pitt and Baldwin and were swept aside by their successors. Should France keep all her conquests and Britain surrender hers? Should Germany be allowed to use self-determination as a lever to destroy Austria and Czechoslovakia with all the consequences for the rest of Europe? Both Addington and Chamberlain saw the issues in terms of immediate needs: peace and breathing space. Only these superficial views can explain their hasty decisions.[27]

There is another quality called specious logic which has contributed to the structure of appeasement. Its arguments are both plausible and false. Invariably its practitioners are voices of moderation: Tom Jones and Lord Lothian before Munich, Sir John Macpherson and Charles Fox at the time of Amiens were its best-known spokesmen.

The Jones-Lothian argument was the essential moderation and reasonableness of Hitler as a German stateman, provided certain grievances were satisfied. "All sorts of people who have met Hitler are convinced that he is a factor for peace," commented Tom Jones.[28] Had not Arnold Toynbee

---

War, 1938–1939 (New York, 1968), pp. 16, 20–21. The misconceptions of the military during the 1930's are described in Laurence Lafore, The end of Glory. An Interpretation of the Origins of World War II (Philadelphia, 1970), pp. 163–167.

[27] There are of course some variations between them. Addington in Commons denied necessity as the reason for peace, and said no better terms could be had two years hence. But Pitt admitted England needed a rest. Chamberlain denied, and many writers have denied him, the argument that Munich granted time to improve England's defenses. While peace was Chamberlain's first object, he was well aware of Britain's military weakness and worked to overcome it.

[28] Thomas Jones, A Diary with Letters, 1931–1950 (London, 1954), p. 125.

returned from a meeting with the Führer "convinced of his sincerity in describing peace in Europe?"[29] Jones would also visit Hitler in search of peace and Anglo-German friendship. In persuading Baldwin to meet with him he pictured the German chancellor as a reasonable man. Lord Lothian, who visited Hitler three times, extended the limits of specious logic far beyond Jones' attempts. Nazi brutality was, so he said, "largely the reflex of the external persecution to which Germans have been subjected since the war."[30]

Addington's England also had its share of dubious reasoning. To illustrate our point one might cite the role of Sir John Macpherson, a former governor general of India, crony of the Prince of Wales and all-round busybody.[31] It is always hard to measure influence, but Macpherson fairly bombarded Addington with hysterical letters in favor of peace.[32] Fundamental to all these messages was the theme that Bonaparte stood for order and peace. He had crushed the Jacobins and now extended the hand of friendship to England. Addington dare not refuse it; a continuation of the war would bring the revolution (i.e. the Jacobins) back, and this time England would not escape it. And to make certain Addington understood, Macpherson assured him: "Bonaparte and his friends are in France what William III was to this country. The Party consolidating government on the rights of property...."[33]

If these arguments strike one as spurious now, they seemed plausible in Addington's day. (Malmesbury was closer to the truth than he realized when he described Macpherson in favor of "conceding steps.") Sir John was a Whig member of parliament and had not the greatest Whig of his day been proclaiming for years that France was the better cause? Charles James Fox

[29] *Ibid.*, pp. 179–182.

[30] As quoted in Thorne, *op. cit.*, p. 16. Not surprising, perhaps, contemporaries nicknamed him "Lord Loathsome."

[31] There are some uncomplimentary portraits of Macpherson by his contemporaries. Lord Glenbervie called him "certainly almost mad," while the Earl of Malmesbury regarded him "an intruding man ... always for conciliatory and conceding steps." Malmesbury, *op. cit.*, IV, p. 246; *The Diaries of Sylvester Douglas, Lord Glenbervie*, ed., by Francis Bickley (London, 1928), I, pp. 300–301.

[32] Early in 1803, Lord Pelham, Home Secretary, lamented to Malmesbury that "Addington had some one (he knew not who) who encouraged him in this system of credulity and retreat..." Was it Macpherson? Malmesbury, *op. cit.*, IV, p. 218.

[33] Pellew, *op. cit.*, in volume I reprinted a few Macpherson letters. In fact, the 1801 and 1802 boxes of the "Addington Papers" hold many more. The quote is from Sir John Macpherson to Henry Addington, October 12, 1802, "Addington Papers," Devon Record Office, Exeter. In a letter of March, 1801, Sir John had stated his conviction "War, continued beyond a certain point, is but the vehicle of interior revolution." Sir John Macpherson to the Earl of Gilford, March 8, 1801, *Ibid.* By September he was warning Addington that "the failure or delay [of peace] would plant the war in our bosom and with it the Revolutionary Revolts." Sir John Macpherson to Henry Addington, September 2, 1801, *Ibid.*

had condemned Pitt and war with France ever since he had adopted the French revolution as his own. Warmhearted, even generous he might be, but on this issue Fox permitted sentiment to outdistance reason. As a consequence, he had to defend his position time and again with dubious logic. When Pitt rejected Bonaparte's first peace offer out of hand (January, 1800), Fox returned to the House of Commons from which he had absented himself since 1797. Denouncing Pitt for continuing the war, he declared: "I shall continue to think and to say ... that this country was the aggressor in the war."[34] By 1801 he was to admit his hatred of the English government as he rejoiced in "the triumph of the French government over the English."[35]

A final touch must be added to our portrait of appeasement. It was provided by a king whose occasional insanity did not affect his political acumen. Almost two months after the peace preliminaries with France had been signed, George III received the Earl of Malmesbury at Windsor. "Do you know what I call the Peace?" he cried out. "An *experimental* Peace, for it is nothing else. I am sure *you* think so, and perhaps do not give it so *gentle* a name ..."[36] It would be hard to improve upon this judgment, for if appeasement was anything, it was experimental. Even Chamberlain in his objective moments had to admit the experimental nature of his approach: he considered a personal visit to Hitler, before it had taken place, "unconventional and daring," he *continued* the policy of rearming Great Britain after the "success" of the Munich conference, and he commented on the cheering crowds who welcomed him back from his third trip to Germany: "All this will be over in three months." As for the phrase "peace for our time," within a week he begged the House of Commons not to take these words too seriously.[37]

It is this experimental quality which has been largely overlooked, and has had to be obscured, perhaps, by the proponents of appeasement. There were so many imponderables, so many risks in dealing with a Bonaparte or a Hitler. Yet war, continued or provoked, was no alternative at all. There had to be another policy, peace must be given every chance. This experimental attitude was of course aided by the fact that, on the short run, appeasement was so much cheaper than war. But overriding even that consideration were the alternatives available to the British ministers if the experiment failed. It is this which made appeasement attractive as a policy. If the experiment mis-

---

[34] Charles James Fox, *Speeches during the French Revolution* (London, 1924), p. 385.

[35] *Memorials and Correspondence of Charles James Fox*, ed. by Lord John Russell (London, 1854), III, p. 349, Charles Fox to Charles Grey, October 22 [1801].

[36] Malmesbury, *op. cit.*, IV, p. 65.

[37] Feiling, *op. cit.*, pp. 357, 381–382; Robbins, *op. cit.*, pp. 330–331.

carried Britain would mobilize, she would go to war and she would arouse her dominion partners. Here lies the weak link in the chain. The experiment was tried and realized with a vengeance. Great Britain had assumed she would have the time to reverse her policies if appeasement collapsed. In fact, she gained little time and barely managed to save herself.

So far we have tried to define appeasement by its own attributes. A broad understanding, however, demands that it be reviewed as a policy too. The appeasement of Hitler, and to a lesser extent of Bonaparte, was carried out against a background of distrust regarding traditional diplomacy. Chamberlain suspected English diplomats because they were critical of his program of reconciliation with Germany. The Foreign Office counseled against appeasement, yet offered no alternatives to those policies which were alleged to have led to World War I. This suspicion of diplomats, shared incidentally by Chamberlain and Hitler, had first encouraged "the visit" by unofficial observers to the Führer. Ultimately, the use of these amateurs (they were free of diplomatic prejudices, but lacked experience and judgment) did much harm. The blunders of appeasement can often be traced to their optimistic and erroneous reports.

The tendency to circumvent regular diplomatic practice also turns up in Addington's time, although the reasons for it are less clear. Perhaps the several failures of the Earl of Malmesbury (1796 in Paris, 1797 at Lisle) to reach a negotiated settlement contributed to it. The "white lion," as he was known, was England's foremost diplomat, but even he did not succeed, despite extensive concessions, in making peace. Attempts to avoid traditional negotiations are quite evident from the efforts of Sir John Macpherson. From a letter to the prime minister we know that he was trying to arrange a personal, informal meeting between M. Otto, the French commissioner in London, and Mr. Addington. This *tête à tête* would avoid the "official" character of the Hawkesbury-Otto negotiations.[38] One further straw in the wind is the appointment of Lord Cornwallis as the British plenipotentiary to conclude the peace treaty with France. Cornwallis had no diplomatic experience at all (he was a general), and the reason for his appointment remains something of a mystery. Addington may have chosen him in order to streng-

---

[38] "Addington Papers," Sir John Macpherson to Henry Addington, May 2, 1801. Macpherson also arranged one or more meetings between Otto and the Prince of Wales, and the latter encouraged Addington in the peace negotiations. *Ibid.*, M. Otto to Sir John Macpherson, January 11, 1802; Pellew, *op. cit.*, II, pp. 24–26, contains a letter of the Prince of Wales to Henry Addington, January 22, 1802. *The Diaries of . . . Lord Glenvervie*, I, pp. 300–301, 310. M. Louis William Otto had been sent to London in 1799, ostensibly to arrange for an exchange of prisoners of war, but Napoleon had given him wide powers to negotiate with England. Ziegler, *op. cit.*, p. 119.

then his ramshackle administration with this high aristocrat (Cornwallis was a marquis). Or, as seems more likely, Cornwallis was sent to Paris to treat with Bonaparte as one general with another. Certainly, no one expected the discussions on the final treaty to last as long as they did.[39]

The criticisms leveled against appeasement have often included the charge that as a policy it was too single-minded. It stood for concessions without alternatives. A closer look will not sustain that charge. The absence of an all-pervasive appeasement – and foreign policy operates on many different levels simultaneously – offers the best proof of that experimental quality which we discussed already. The model of appeasement provides several instances of concessions competing with other methods of foreign policy.

Addington, who assumed office as prime minister in March, 1801, opened peace talks at once. At the same time he persisted in an active prosecution of the war; that same month Sir Ralph Abercromby drove the French from Egypt, and in April Admiral Nelson overwhelmed the Danish fleet before Copenhagen. Negotiations had hardly gotten underway then, but in late July and early August when those hung in the balance, Nelson bombarded, without much success, the barges in the harbor of Boulogne. Appeasement or not, the chances for invasion had to be frustrated.[40] Since England and France were still at war, Nelson's actions were justified and had the support of the government; besides, his raids did not even interrupt the efforts for peace on either side.

Although the historical reputation of the Chamberlain government rests largely on its appeasement policies, it is also true that it did not pursue its peace objectives in a single-minded fashion. On the long way to Munich there were side-roads which the Cabinet took in the search for peace. One of these alternate routes was used frequently: the British government warned Hitler time and again that the use of force to solve the Czech problem might result in war, and once the fighting started no one could predict what would happen. If such warnings over a period of months rang hollow, this was at least in part due to an inflated notion of their value. Great Britain lived on its reputation, and the English government believed that if it issued a carefully worded admonition, whether backed by force or not, it would receive the right attention.

From March till September, 1938, it rained *caveats* on the German government: Chamberlain spoke in Parliament on March 24, a warning was given in

---

[39] At first a seasoned diplomat, Lord Whitworth, had apparently been chosen to go to France to negotiate. See Malmesbury, *op. cit.*, IV, p. 54.

[40] "Addington Papers," Lord Nelson to Henry Addington, August 4, 1801; *Letters of . . . the Earl of St. Vincent*, I, p. 134, Earl of St. Vincent to Lord Nelson, August 11, 1801.

Berlin during the May crisis, in July the prime minister and his foreign secretary expressed their concern that Germany might use force, and in late August the chancellor of the exchequer, Sir John Simon, at the direction of the prime minister, delivered another warning in a speech at Lanark. When disturbances in the Sudetenland in early September seemed to invite German intervention, Lord Halifax was sufficiently concerned to instruct the British ambassador to warn Hitler of the consequences of a war. Sir Nevile Henderson convinced the foreign secretary, however, that this move would be unwise and his instructions were withdrawn. Finally, during the height of the Munich crisis Great Britain mobilized her fleet and on September 26 issued a strong communiqué promising British support for France should a peaceful settlement fail.

All such incidents are too well-known to need elaboration, but how can they be explained for a government singularly determined on appeasement? It has been customary to regard England's leaders as hypocritical and insincere (not to mention worse), but these are portraits in black and white. Moreover, our concern here is not with the efficacy of appeasement but with its place in the total foreign policy of Great Britain. Not even Chamberlain in advocating "appeasement of the world" would have endorsed it as the only line of policy, and it never was. The many warnings given Germany in 1938 demonstrate that the British government was prepared to consider alternatives to appeasement, even if it doubted their wisdom or feasibility.[41]

When the scales of decision eventually tip in favor of appeasement, the choice is hesitant and hardly free of doubt. Appeasement as policy generated no conviction, only delusions, which Christopher Thorne has dignified with another name.

> Appeasement became a mission. How many can believe in their mission whilst leaving unimpaired their judgment, their acceptance of criticism . . . ? Missions can corrupt as much as power, and Chamberlain, with his "inexhaustible vanity," found both to his liking.[42]

To convert doubt into misguided zeal may be human, but it should, nevertheless, be recognized for what it is: for Addington or Chamberlain to take the path of appeasement was a gambler's throw, a deliberate leap into uncertainty. In conversation with Rufus King, the American minister in London, Addington admitted that "neither success nor adversity" would

[41] Donald N. Lammers, *Explaining Munich: The Search for Motive in British Policy* (Stanford, 1966), *passim*. Lammers arrived at fairly similar conclusions, though he dealt only with the Russian and communist aspects of appeasement. The quote is from Feiling, *op. cit.*, p. 355.

[42] Thorne, *op. cit.*, p. 20.

change his wish for peace, but "in respect to the negotiations, they seemed perpetually approaching without being any nearer." These sentiments, voiced in May, 1801, were echoed ten months later, when the signing of the definitive treaty was overdue and the prime minister showed no more certitude.

Addington in a pretty free conversation told me that during the last fortnight his mind had balanced whether to wish the conclusion or rupture of the negotiation; that he was every day receiving letters expressive of the same indecision from all parts of the kingdom . . . [43]

Suffice it to add that Pitt, in conversation with the Earl of Malmesbury, expressed a similar uncertainty about Bonaparte's intentions.[44]

In the twentieth century, when so much more could be known about Hitler and Nazi Germany, Chamberlain chose not to face the facts. He had read *The House that Hitler Built*, but "if I accepted the author's conclusions, I should despair, but I don't and won't."[45] Rather, he couldn't, for what indeed had prepared his Victorian mind to deal with the realities of the Nazi revolution? We know how desperately he longed for peace, but is that equivalent to a mission? What pulled Chamberlain the other way, what made him doubt Hitler's good intentions, were his business instincts which knew how to balance investments versus risks. Vincent Massey has preserved an image of Chamberlain after the Godesberg conference: "determined to avoid war if possible, but not confident of success." And the prime minister "had reluctantly come to the conclusion that Hitler's profession of limited objectives was not sincere . . ."[46] After this he went to Munich.

Why, then, do Addington and Chamberlain go on to conclude agreements? For one, the thrust of the policies which they had initiated could not so easily be reversed. Each prime minister was also impelled by the need for success and showed a willingness "to go to absurd lengths" for the sake of peace.[47] Finally, both Addington and Chamberlain had succeeded in deceiving themselves and were confused about what was real and what they wished to be real. Taken together, these factors drove them on, perhaps even against their better instincts.

[43] *The . . . Correspondence of Rufus King*, III, pp. 443–444, IV, p. 81, Rufus King to Secretary of State, March 13, 1802.

[44] Malmesbury, *op. cit.*, IV, pp. 67–68.

[45] Feiling, *op. cit.*, p. 328. The conclusions, in brief, were that war with Hitler was inevitable.

[46] Vincent Massey was the Canadian High Commissioner in London. He gathered these impressions at a meeting of the Dominion High Commissioners and the prime minister, after the latter's return from his second flight to Germany. The quotes are in Robbins, *op cit.*, pp. 299–300. See also the comments of A. J. P. Taylor, *English History, 1914–1945*, vol. XV of *The Oxford History of England* (Oxford, 1965), p. 431.

[47] The phrase is Tom Jones', *op cit.*, p. 396, March 20, 1938.

Did appeasement as a policy make England's enemies aware of her pacific intentions? It certainly did; it did it all too well! The inadequacy of appeasement is the inadequacy to communicate clearly how far this policy would go. Thus, what was seen as the final concession on the one side was regarded as the first in a series of triumphs by the other. Sir Orme Sargent of the British foreign office realized this clearly – after the event.

> ... although Hitler was not propitiated, I do believe that he was deceived by our servile act of abnegation [at Munich]. ...How could he, poor man, have been expected to understand that this grovelling gesture of ours signified on the contrary that the worm was at last going to make ready to turn.[48]

There is cause to suggest that Bonaparte's policies, after the conclusion of peace with Great Britain, followed a similar line of conduct. In February, 1801, the First Consul had signed a peace treaty with Austria which included the recognition of the Dutch (Batavian), Swiss (Helvetian) and two Italian (Cisalpine and Ligurian) republics. The Addington cabinet naively assumed that these provisions need not be repeated in its agreement with Bonaparte; i.e., the English saw the Austrian treaty and their own compact with him as forming a comprehensive European settlement. Only inexperience and failure to comprehend Napoleon's ambitions can explain Addington's error.

The First Consul not only refused to admit any connection between the pact with Austria and the one with England; he sought to restrict Britain to her island without any voice in European affairs. Between the signing of the preliminaries (October 1, 1801) and the conclusion of the definitive treaty (March 27, 1802), he arranged his election as executive of the Cisalpine government with the title of president of the *Italian* republic. The English were severely shaken and Lord Hawkesbury, the Foreign Secretary, denounced the "inordinate ambition, the gross breach of faith and the inclination to insult Europe."[49] The English government then indicated its continued interest in peace by signing a treaty two months later which confirmed the substantial concessions of the preliminaries. Of course Bonaparte was impressed, but the wrong way. His next violations of the European "settlement" were the continued occupation of the Dutch republic by French troops, and his interference in the domestic affairs of Switzerland in the fall of 1802.[50] England's policies had completely failed to indicate how far she

---

[48] Sir Orme Sargent to J. W. Wheeler-Bennett, [December 30, 1946], in Gilbert, *Roots of Appeasement*, pp. 222–223.

[49] As quoted in Arthur Bryant, *The Years of Endurance, 1793–1802* (London, 1942), p. 349.

[50] "I declare to you," Napoleon told the Swiss deputies assembled in Paris, "that I would rather sacrifice a 100,000 men than to suffer that England should mix in your affairs, for, if one

would permit Napoleon to go, and she soon regretted having conceded so much (as e.g. the evacuation of Malta). If appeasement finally decided it had had enough, its beneficiary's appetite had merely been whetted.

As a policy appeasement was something of an anomaly. Although the elements of appeasement had been part of diplomacy for a long time, when joined into a policy it was uncertain, ineffective and a gamble – qualities usually not recommended for diplomacy. These variations from the norm may be due to the revolutionary times in which diplomats had to practice their *métier*. But then, these difficult times also created a certain outlook which may be as responsible. An aura of pessimism hangs over the appeasers, and their mood has established appeasement likewise as a state of mind.

Marquis Cornwallis, the "tragic hero" of Yorktown and negotiator at Amiens, will serve as a case in point. From the first he was "gloomy" about the war with France, feared the chances for a revolution at home, and exclaimed: "would to God that we had peace almost on any terms, for it is evident that we cannot make war."[51] On the eve of his departure for France to negotiate a treaty he confessed to being "out of sorts, low-spirited, and tired of everything . . ."[52] If representative of anything, Cornwallis' fatigue faithfully mirrored the condition of the British people in 1801. England needed a rest, and whether the war could be won or not, was it worth to go on fighting? Addington did not think so and told the Commons that better terms could not be had.[53]

That appeasement was as much a state of mind as a policy, owing to an attitude of pessimism about England's position and condition, can hardly be disputed when one measures the political atmosphere of the 1930's. One might call it a loss of nerve, or the qualms of conscience about the prior treatment of Germany; one could refer to Britain's lack of military preparations and the absence of the money for it; and some, like Mussolini, gratuitously were of the opinion that the "tired sons" of rich fathers lacked the

---

official word, be it in the London Gazette or in the diplomatic relations, had been given out by the cabinet of St. James, the question would have been settled – I would have united you to France." [February, 1803], as quoted in Deutsch, *op. cit.*, p. 92.

[51] *Correspondence of Charles, First Marquis Cornwallis*, ed. by Charles Ross (London, 1859), II, p. 259, Cornwallis to Charles Ross, August 25, 1794; p. 328, same to same, December 15, 1797; III, p. 292, same to same, September 17, 1800.

[52] *Ibid.*, III, p. 382, Cornwallis to Ross, September 17, 1801. If a professional soldier, former governor general of India, and lord lieutenant of Ireland felt this way, how many other people in government or outside of it held similar views? Sir John Macpherson was certainly one of them.

[53] *Parliamentary History of England*, XXXVI, pp. 768, 812–814. The Foreign Secretary, Lord Hawkesbury, admitted in the same debate on the definitive treaty that "peace was called for loudly by the country." *Ibid.*, XXXVI, p. 758.

ability to continue Britain's imperial traditions.[54] Each reason said essentially the same thing: Great Britain appeared to have lost the will to fight. In November, 1937, Harold Nicolson noted in his diary: "Tory opinion is almost entirely on the run and would willingly let Germany take Russia and over-run the Near East so long as she leaves us alone." (This according to Duncan Sandys whom he had seen.)[55] After the demise of Austria he learned from Malcolm MacDonald, Secretary of State for the Dominions, how weak Britain's defenses really were.

All we can do is by wise retreat and good diplomacy to diminish the dangers being arrayed against us. The Cabinet know full well that we are shirking great responsibility. But they cannot undertake such responsibility.[56]

As a state of mind appeasement could at least pretend to be "realistic."

Appeasement, as it has been defined in these pages, primarily means the British version. This being the case, our analysis can only be complete after certain specifically English contributions are taken into account. The first of these is the conventions of parliament and the parliamentary turn of mind. Other countries have parliaments, but in England its traditions were of such long standing that certain behavior patterns in official business were accepted without question. Among these were negotiating procedures of give and take resulting eventually in compromise, the absence of threats, fair play, and the conviction that an opponent who had given his word (and put his signature) on an agreement could be expected to stand by it. Diplomacy has its own set of rules which showed perhaps greater realism about "sharp practive." But neither Addington and Hawkesbury, nor Chamberlain and Halifax were seasoned diplomats.[57] Their parliamentary experience had not prepared them for the international arena, to meet a Bonaparte, Hitler or Mussolini, where they must negotiate under conditions of dynamic stress and willful deceit.

The trimming ways of appeasement are thus not only the symptoms of fear, or result exclusively from military weakness, but owe an important measure

---

[54] *The Ciano Diaries, 1939–1943*, ed. by Hugh Gibson (New York, 1946), p. 10, January 11, 1939.

[55] Harold Nicolson, *Diaries and Letters, 1930–1939*, Vol. I (London, 1966), p. 313, November 18, 1937.

[56] *Ibid.*, I, p. 333, March 29, 1938. See also Gilbert and Gott, *The Appeasers*, p. 5 who call "appeasement . . . an attitude of mind . . ."

[57] Addington had no experience beyond the House of Commons; Hawkesbury had travelled in Europe; Chamberlain had some international experience, for he had participated in the 1932 Lausanne Conference which ended German reparations, and Halifax had been Viceroy of India and President of the Board of Education.

to the parliamentary manner. But the tendency to bargain and compromise, to weigh the advantages and calculate costs came from other sources too. England's business attitudes should not be overlooked in the effort at a definition of appeasement. The business ethos was especially strong in Neville Chamberlain who regarded Germany as "a rising market" and wanted to "sit down at a table with the Germans and run through all their complaints and claims with a pencil ..."[58] There were no businessmen in Addington's cabinet, but the views of the business community (especially in London, and Pitt was close to the City) cannot have been unknown to him. Business circles wanted peace and trade, and would sacrifice much to get both. The merchants and manufacturers of Manchester petitioned the prime minister to seek the reopening of the European market which remained closed to British goods, even after the peace preliminaries had been signed.[59] Elsewhere, Edward Baines, editor of the *Leeds Mercury*, was convinced that the war was ruining Britain's new industry. "... Nothing but the restoration of peace could save the country," he explained.[60]

An even more plausible English contribution to appeasement can be found in the empirical and pragmatic frame of mind. Both qualities – experimentation and practicality – are central to the British experience: empiricism had developed into a philosophical principle, pragmatism was equated with virtue. It had taken centuries for each to become firmly rooted in English ways. The absence of any ideological commitment in foreign affairs was very useful for appeasement in the short run and proved fatal for its reputation later on.[61] Free from ideological considerations, England could placate continental tyrants regardless of her domestic convictions. Did this flexibility confer any advantage? Not really, because it led to concessions which ignored such international principles as the balance of power, the rights of small states, and even Britain's own interests. The rejection of any ideological commitment also led Chamberlain into great moral confusion. In the hope of righting past wrongs he participated in an even worse injustice: the partition of Czechoslovakia. Addington followed a rather similar line when he abandoned the Dutch, the two Italian and the Swiss republics to Bonaparte so that

[58] Feiling, *op. cit.*, p. 329; Gilbert and Gott, *The Appeasers*, p. 52.

[59] "Addington Papers," Devon Record Office, 1802 box, "A Petition of the Merchants and Manufacturers of Manchester," April 26, 1802.

[60] *Leeds Mercury*, October 17, 1801, "Editorial," and quoted in Donald Read, *Press and People, 1790–1850; Opinion in three English cities* (London, 1961), pp. 77, 108.

[61] Stanley Baldwin especially feared the divisive influence of foreign affairs on the domestic scene. See Northedge, *op. cit.*, pp. 385–386, 440–441.

England might have peace.[62] Whatever good intentions appeasement may have had in mind, such excesses bankrupted it as a policy.

Finally, England's diplomatic style may have contributed its share. The tendency to eschew "all or nothing" policies, an inclination to tolerance and moderation, and a habit of caution: these are the elements that aided the course of appeasement.[63] Nor are these characteristics to be despised, though they were misinterpreted when put to use appeasing Bonaparte or Hitler. Yet, if one considers the visions of these tempestuous figures, the prosaic hopes of appeasement had small chance of success in any case.

[62] On the lack of principle and appeasement, Wheeler-Bennett, *Munich*, pp. 3–8; A. L. Rowse, *Appeasement: A Study in Political Decline, 1933–1939* (New York, 1961), p. 116 states "In this story [i.e. of appeasement] we see the decadence of British empiricism, empiricism carried beyond all rhyme or reason." On Chamberlain's moral confusion, see Lafore, *The End of Glory*, pp. 232–233.

[63] See the comments of Sir Harold Nicolson about British diplomatic style in Sir Harold Nicolson, *Diplomacy*, 2nd ed. (London, 1955), pp. 127–144.

CHAPTER III

ON MOTIVES AND SIMILARITIES

Without motives appeasement would make no sense at all, unless one is determined to regard it as sheer cowardice or mindless surrender. Since simplistic explanations offer so little in the way of an answer, the search for motives might prove more fruitful. But motive is an elusive quality too, difficult to document or "prove," and always hard to relate to specific decisions or events. It is not even possible to assume that all motives fall neatly into one category.

For our purposes, at least, it is elementary to distinguish between personal motives and what might be called "motives (i.e., reasons) of state." This is not meant to deny the existence of class or other group motives, lying in the realm between the individual and the state. A general interpretation of appeasement will fail, however, along class lines, even if this or that individual may have been motivated by such interests. The policies of appeasement cut across too many social lines, and caused enough strain within each group, that it could never qualify as a class instrument.[1]

Despite this limitation, the motives of our two categories span broadly enough to cover a multitude of factors. Personal motives for appeasement include both fear and guilt, and can look vague or uncertain in their make-up. Motives of state, on the other hand, appear definite or specific and without fail deal with military or economic matters. In speaking of motives one other consideration should be kept in view. Appeasement of Napoleon and Hitler was the pragmatic, conservative response to a revolutionary age, and these revolutionary times, which we mentioned already, must have exercised a powerful influence on all motivations. What would barely pass as motive in ordinary days might be greatly intensified in a disturbed period.

In analyzing motives of state or specific reasons for appeasement first,

---

[1] A. L. Rowse, *Appeasement: A Study in Political Decline, 1933–1939* (New York, 1961), especially pp. 117–119 emphasizes class interests as responsible for appeasement. This explanation was criticized as untenable by George A. Lanyi, "The Problem of Appeasement," *World Politics*, XV (January, 1963), pp. 325–326.

military factors should be at the head of the list. A state which feels secure militarily does not turn to appeasement, even if it wishes to compromise. Great Britain was not so fortunate at the time of Amiens and Munich. Her military situation was different in 1938 from 1801, yet came to the same dilemma: her military capacities were inadequate for the challenges and dangers which she faced. At least, her leaders and many others thought this was the case and said so. [2]

How could military conditions be different and the reaction be the same? Since 1793 Great Britain had been at war with revolutionary France. Despite repeated naval victories and colonial conquests at the expense of the French, Dutch and Spanish empires, she had lost the war in Europe itself. In 1795 her armies had had to evacuate the Low Countries and British soldiers did not return to the European continent for more than a decade. Expeditions to Holland in 1799 and the Iberian peninsula in 1800 failed badly. She might win in Egypt but could not defeat the French republic, governed after November, 1799 by Bonaparte. Resistance to England in the Baltic by the "Armed Neutrality" of the northern powers, and a growing conflict with Russia threatened her military posture after 1800. While her difficulties mounted, England won battles at Alexandria and Copenhagen and lost her last allies (Austria and Portugal) to France. Clearly, the total military contest was beyond her and by 1801 she was gradually being exhausted. Bonaparte had talked peace while waging war, but Great Britain only listened when military necessity motivated her to do so.

The pause Great Britain needed in 1801 had come again with the Armistice of 1918. Four years of strenuous fighting were followed by twenty years of peace. Moreover, the British government permitted its defense policies to be

---

[2] In 1801 Great Britain had to refuse a call for military assistance from Portugal, her last ally on the Continent, because it was "...not in the power of your Majesty, consistent with a due regard to the safety of your Kingdom." *The Later Correspondence of George III*, ed. by A. Aspinall (Cambridge, 1967), III, p. 511, Cabinet minute [1801, Lord Hawkesbury's handwriting]. "...In our wooden walls alone must we place our trust; we should make a sad business of it on shore," wrote Marquis Cornwallis that same year. *Correspondence of Charles, First Marquis Cornwallis*, ed. by Charles Ross (London, 1859), III, p. 380, Cornwallis to Ross, August 4, 1801. Lord Minto, after a conversation with the King, concluded that, as a result of Pitt's resignation, "the prosecution of the war became perhaps impossible..." *The Paget Papers* (London, 1896), I, p. 29, Lord Minto to the Hon. A. Paget, January 4, 1802. The Chiefs of Staff reported to the government on March 22, 1938 that Britain was not ready for war and that it was essential to gain time. Keith Robbins, *Munich, 1938* (London, 1968), p. 201. Robbins gives the date as March 28. See, however, Keith Middlemas, *The Diplomacy of Illusion: The British Government and Germany, 1937–39* (London, 1972), pp. 192–193 and Ian Colvin, *The Chamberlain Cabinet* (New York, 1971), pp. 111–112. The future Chief of the Imperial General Staff, General Ironside, noted in his diary just before Munich that Chamberlain was "right," for exposure to a German attack would be suicidal. Quoted in W. N. Medlicott, *British Foreign Policy since Versailles, 1919–1963* (London, 1968), p. 181.

based on the assumption that it would not have to face a major war in the next ten years. This decision was made informally in 1919, and reviewed annually by the Committee of Imperial Defence. By 1928 the ten-year clause became a formal rule, and although abolished in 1932, it took until March 1935 for rearmament to become once more the established policy.[3] This fifteen year period of unilateral disarmament left Britain in a very inferior military condition. In July, 1934 the British air force had only half the strength of the French air arm and four fifth of the Italian one. No one knew the exact strength of the German air force, but it did exist and had aircraft more modern than the British planes.[4]

Britain's military inferiority was not just in the air, however, but in each service branch her fighting strength was well below the 1914 levels. World War I had left her exhausted in many ways, and the failure to remain properly armed was only the most tangible expression of this fatigue. The entire concept of war as a viable policy was under attack, and this too showed how tired the British people were of fighting. Excessive armaments were blamed for the genesis of the world war, and war was denounced as failing to solve any problems. In this atmosphere rearmament could not proceed rapidly but appeasement thrived.

One other point can be made in the comparative context of military reasons for appeasement. Seemingly minor decisions in military planning and traditional approaches to strategy contributed much to Britain's option for appeasement. Where the war with revolutionary France was concerned, Pitt's strategical decisions were so deficient that Great Britain almost lost the war outright. Since the initial campaign of 1793–1795 was bungled by the Duke of York, Pitt reverted to England's traditional form of warfare. While the navy swept the oceans free of enemy ships and took its colonies, allies were subsidized to fight England's battles in Europe. Pitt also attempted to crush France financially.[5] All these efforts at limited warfare failed, and Pitt's successor was faced with the choice of appeasing Bonaparte or total war.[6]

[3] Robbins, *op. cit.*, pp. 96–99.

[4] F. S. Northedge, *The Troubled Giant. Great Britain Among the Great Powers, 1916–1939* (New York, 1966), p. 387.

[5] See the contemporary estimate of William Wilberforce, *The Life of William Wilberforce*, by his sons Robert Isaac and Samuel Wilberforce (London, 1838), II, pp. 91–92. Pitt's financial warfare led one observer to ask: "I should like to know who was Chancellor of the Exchequer to Atilla." *Ibid.*, II, p. 92 footnote.

[6] J. Steven Watson, *The Reign of George III, 1760–1815, The Oxford History of England*, vol. 12 (Oxford, 1960), pp. 373–374; A. W. Ward and G. P. Gooch, ed., *The Cambridge History of British Foreign Policy, 1783–1919* (Cambridge, 1939), I, pp. 265–266. See also the perceptive comments of Edward Ingram, "British Strategy and High Command, 1783–1819: a Bibliographical Review," *Militärgeschichtliche Mitteilungen*, No. 2 (1972), pp. 165–172.

Similar tactical decisions, though perhaps of a more technical nature, had enormous military importance in the twentieth century. Much like Pitt's government followed traditional policies once the campaign against revolutionary France had failed in Europe, so England's leaders (both civilian and military) increasingly viewed rearmament in a traditional light. Following the lessons of World War I, a definite preference for defensive over offensive strategy began to surface. In terms of air power this meant an emphasis on the fighter over the bomber. While the fear of a sudden attack from the air makes this policy understandable, the concentration on England's defensive requirements reduced her military influence in Europe to zero. For Austria, Czechoslovakia or Poland the slow increase in British fighter aircraft carried little comfort; most of Germany was beyond the range of fighter planes in 1938, and without bombers Great Britain could exert no real military pressure on the Berlin government.[7]

It would be too much to say that the statesmen responsible for rearmament in the 1930's really understood the results of their fears: that rearmament emphasizing defense could no more save Britain from appeasement than Pitt's methods of limited warfare had prevented it before. In either case the consequences of indecisive or poor strategic planning led to the abandonment of the European continent as a theater of operations. Once this had taken place appeasement was all but inevitable.

Beyond the specific military motives for appeasement are the equally substantial material ones. War, or getting ready for war, demands so much in human and material terms that if the national will to either purpose fails, the burden of preparedness or of fighting becomes too much and is rejected for less forceful policies. Once again we must cast a wide net in order to detect the comparative significance of the material motives for appeasement.

William Pitt had become prime minister in 1783 when England's fortunes were at a low ebb following the loss of the American colonies. For ten years he presided over a "national revival" and enacted significant administrative and financial reforms.[8] This recovery had been achieved through strict economy and a reduction in the armed forces as late as 1792. Pitt's expertise was finance, and though he may have accepted war with France too readily in 1793, the cost of the long struggle must have appalled him. The English national debt amounted to £230 million in 1793; by 1802 when peace

---

[7] Robbins, *op. cit.*, pp. 201–202 has a detailed discussion of the implications of the fighter versus the bomber. See also Middlemas, *Diplomacy of Illusion*, p. 221 who emphasizes the financial considerations which led to the preference of the fighter plane over the bomber.

[8] J. H. Rose, *William Pitt and National Revival* (London, 1911), *passim*.

returned it had reached the unthinkable figure of £ 507 million.[9] Twice in the last quarter of the eighteenth century Britain had fought debilitating and ultimately losing wars.

It is true that England's economy expanded during the war with France and her export trade increased each year. But neither the growth in the national debt nor in the volume of her export trade gave an accurate picture of the totality of war's impact on British life. There was a rash of bank failures and bankruptcies in 1793; by 1795 the increased costs of provisions led to food riots in the summer and the King was shot at in October on his way to open Parliament. Two years later England appeared on the verge of collapse. Pitt's policy of subsidizing his allies with gold had failed to defeat revolutionary France but nearly destroyed the national credit and the Bank of England. The Bank was forced to suspend payments in gold and had to issue £ 1 and £ 2 paper notes instead. In the ensuing period the British government resorted to ever more burdensome taxes on windows, wigs, servants, carriages, and finally on income itself to finance the desperate struggle with France. Pitt trebled and even quadrupled the assessed taxes. By 1801, when he resigned and Addington made peace, food riots (partly the result of bad harvests) were convulsing England from one end to the other.

Sir Arthur Bryant admits that Pitt was wrong on two accounts: he "remained unshakably convinced that the defeat of France would be achieved through the economic strength of Britain."[10] Moreover, as disciple of Adam Smith he believed that he could shift the major costs of the war through heavy borrowing to the next generation. As long as he provided the foundations for England's commercial wealth, the burden would seem light for later Englishmen. He was dangerously mistaken on the short run, though correct from a longer perspective. Since his contemporaries could only appreciate (or suffer) the consequences of his short term errors, the inadequacy of Pitt's economic warfare, and of the attempt to relieve his countrymen of the costs of the war, contributed much to the nation's determination to end the war once he had left office.

It is not necessary to search for similar economic motives in the twentieth century; its participants have left us the records of their decisions. The ravages of World War I left deep scars everywhere; though Great Britain was spared an invasion she suffered no less. Her losses in men and wealth, in foreign markets and investments, in useful production, resources and ships

[9] Geoffrey Bruun, *Europe and the French Imperium, 1799–1814* (New York, 1938), pp. 100–101.

[10] Arthur Bryant, *The Years of Endurance, 1793–1802*, Fontana books edit. (London, 1961), p. 167.

were too large to comprehend. The end of the war did not bring back the prosperous times which might have repaired the economic damage. Britain had been slipping economically even before 1914; now a rigid monetary policy hindered her economic recovery and rendered her export position more difficult in the face of foreign competition. A permanent pall of unemployment, or underemployment, settled over the British economy. A full return to pre-war prosperity had not been achieved when ten years after the peace treaty the Great Depression produced severe dislocation and unemployment.

From the standpoint of domestic stability and orthodox economics Great Britain may be called successful in dealing with the consequences of the depression. When the Labor government of Ramsay MacDonald proved unequal to the task of saving the nation's credit and economy, it was replaced by a National government, still headed by MacDonald but controlled by Stanley Baldwin, the leader of the Conservative party. The economy and its recovery was taken firmly in hand by Neville Chamberlain, the new Chancellor of the Exchequer. Chamberlain managed to balance the budget through sharp cuts in governmental spending, a sure sign of orthodoxy. An indication that the worst of the depression was over came in 1935 when unemployment fell again below two million.[11]

England's limited recovery, remarkable though it was, took its toll. There was of course the obvious in human suffering, frustration and unfulfilled ambitions, and the unexpected like the naval mutiny at Invergordon. But the most serious price paid for economic recovery was first the reluctance and then the hesitancy with which Britain began to rearm. Stanley Baldwin, prime minister after June 1935, hesitated to tell the voters about the country's military needs. "I give you my word there will be no great armaments," he announced in the election campaign of 1935.[12] Yet six months before a White Paper on national defense had publicized the government's intention to rearm, be it ever so slowly.

Baldwin was much more involved in defense matters than was previously known, but the routine tasks of rearmament fell on the shoulders of the Chancellor of the Exchequer who would have to find the money for it. Neville Chamberlain did not oppose rearmament: he had wanted to fight the 1935 election on this issue but had been overruled. Still, he approached rearmament with some peculiar views. For one, he abhorred war and would go to very great lengths to avoid it. Given this attitude, Chamberlain did not view

---

[11] David Thomson, *England in the Twentieth Century*, The Pelican History of England: 9 (London, 1965), p. 144.

[12] As quoted in Keith Feiling, *The Life of Neville Chamberlain* (London, 1946), p. 269.

rearmament as preparation for a possible war, but as strengthening Britain's defensive position in the negotiation of a settlement which would avert a conflict. What was even more crucial, he refused to endanger Britain's economic recovery by a rapid build-up of her defenses:

If we were now to follow Winston's [Churchill] advice and sacrifice our commerce to the manufacture of arms, we should inflict a certain injury on our trade from which it would take generations to recover, we should destroy the confidence which now happily exists, and we should cripple the revenue . . . [13]

Chamberlain received strong support for this economic impediment to rearmament from Sir Warren Fisher, the permanent Under-Secretary of the Treasury. Sir Warren, occupying the highest civil service position in the Treasury during the 1930's, saw modern war in such economic terms that Great Britain could not possibly be in a military position to negotiate from strength for years. In the words of D. C. Watt:

In Fisher's view, the total nature of modern war made success in it dependent not only upon the effective use of national resources but on their care and maintenance. The Treasury, in his view, became a kind of additional Service department. Finance was the fourth arm of war. Without economic stability, which meant the continued capacity to obtain supplies from abroad and the best use of Britain's manpower and industrial resources, Britain's defeat was inevitable. [14]

The economic views of these two men seem oddly reminiscent of Pitt's unshakable belief that Great Britain's economic strength could defeat revolutionary France. In more stable times these opinions might have proved correct, but for warfare in a revolutionary age the use of economic strategies were simply not sufficient. It left Great Britain exhausted in 1801 and inadequately armed in 1938. Her subsequent foreign policy was a counterpart of the admission that economic considerations lay at the roots of her military insufficiency.

Is appeasement the way in which a government indicates that the costs of power are too much for it to bear? At certain times the answer would appear to be yes. In such periods of contraction, when power (or greatness, the popular equivalent) is not prized, cabinets are obliged to limit their commitments and expenditures. For William Windham, secretary at war in Pitt's

[13] *Ibid.*, p. 314. For Baldwin's contributions to rearmament, and the differences between his position and Chamberlain's, as to its role in England's foreign policy, see Keith Middlemas and John Barnes, *Baldwin. A Biography* (New York, 1970), especially pp. 1025–1026.

[14] D. C. Watt, "Sir Warren Fisher and British rearmament against Germany," in D. C. Watt, *Personalities and Policies. Studies in the Formulation of British Foreign Policy in the Twentieth Century* (South Bend, 1965), p. 113.

cabinet and outspoken disciple of Burke, Addington's peace preliminaries were the end of greatness. It was all over with Great Britain, he told the House of Commons.[15] "We have sustained a total and unmitigated defeat," said Churchill in the same place after the Munich conference.[16] Both men challenged the general mood of the day when, with brave words, they sought to rouse the spirit of a more valiant Britain.

Insofar as the failure to pay the costs of power leads to appeasement, it must be regarded as a specific economic motive. In the light of public opinion, which was tired of war in 1801 and not ready for it in 1938 (being still tired from World War I), the cabinet believed it was following the correct policy. Neither Addington nor Chamberlain can be described as formidable leaders. Ultimately, therefore, the trend toward limiting the costs of power was a reflection of their society, the resources it was willing to mobilize, and their own limitations.

In searching for specific motives for appeasement, the state of international affairs and the balance of power must also be taken into account. It cannot be denied that the realities of the international situation did not favor Great Britain in 1801 or 1938. When she joined the struggle against revolutionary France, England, Austria, Prussia, Holland and Spain constituted the First Coalition. By 1795 its campaigns in Europe had been frustrated; English soldiers were evacuating the continent as Holland was occupied by French troops, and the First Coalition began to crumble. Despite English subsidies, Prussia signed a peace treaty with France, Spain did likewise and Holland became the Batavian republic. Only Austria remained to fight France on land. In 1797 she signed the treaty of Campo Formio to end the fighting. The French republic had overcome its enemies, except for England.

For three years she fought on alone, under the most trying circumstances at home and abroad. Pitt's Second Coalition enlisted the aid of Russia, Austria, Naples, Portugal and the Ottoman empire. Formed in 1798, three years and several unsuccessful campaigns later it lay in ruins. But this time Great Britain was not simply deserted by her allies; some of them turned against her. Since 1795 Prussia had maintained a suspicious neutrality in northern Germany, perhaps inhibited by French promises about Hanover which was still subject to George III. Russia broke with the Second Coalition in 1800. Paul may have been tempted by Bonaparte's plans, but Austrian treachery and English high-handedness played a more important part in his decision. In his anger at a former ally (Britain rather than Russia had secured Malta) Paul

---

[15] *The Parliamentary History of England from the Earliest Period to the Year 1803* (London, 1820), XXXVI, pp. 87–92.

[16] Winston S. Churchill, *The Gathering Storm* (Boston, 1948), p. 326.

revived the League of Armed Neutrality against England. Prussia, Sweden and Denmark joined the Tsar in the attempt to stop the arbitrary habit of British cruisers in searching neutral vessels.[17]

When Austria made peace with France in February, 1801, and Prussia occupied Hanover, it seemed that England could not continue the struggle for long. The entire continent would soon be closed to her. Then, within two weeks, three widely separated events improved her situation once more. On March 21 an English army defeated a French one in Egypt, three days later Paul I was murdered in a palace coup, and on April 2 Admiral Nelson destroyed the Danish fleet before Copenhagen. The last two events smashed the League of Armed Neutrality and relieved Great Britain from anxiety about northern Europe. While French diplomacy had suffered a setback, England nevertheless remained alone in her contest with Bonaparte. Friends and allies she had not, but enemies and envious neutrals there were.[18]

While England, after an exhausting war, was utterly alone against Bonaparte, her situation in 1938 did not seem to be as bleak. Yet the impression was deceiving. In the opinion of those responsible for policy her position was not much better. The effects of World War I had hardly faded when the Depression introduced widespread unemployment and hardship in Great Britain. The ubiquitous social question alone would restrain the cabinet from assuming foreign commitments which might be repudiated by the electorate.[19]

A quick survey of the major states in Europe and beyond during the 1930's furnished the English government with little cause for optimism. Who could be counted on to aid her if Great Britain chose to challenge the ambitions of Nazi Germany? The Soviet Union? France? The United States? Italy? Japan? Wherever the cabinet turned it was confronted with difficulties and of course its own doubts.

Although Winston Churchill more than once advised the government to open discussions for an agreement with Russia against Germany, Chamber-

---

[17] Bruun, op. cit., p. 43.

[18] Prussia reluctantly evacuated Hanover when the League of Armed Neutrality had failed. It has been pointed out already that George III was inclined to accept the peace preliminaries because his allies had deserted him. *Diaries and Correspondence of James Harris, First Earl of Malmesbury*, ed. by the third Earl (London, 1845), IV, p. 65. The significance of the victory in Egypt is spelled out by Edward Ingram, "A Preview of the Great Game in Asia – III: the Origins of the British Expedition to Egypt in 1801," *Middle Eastern Studies*, 9 (October 1973), pp. 296–314.

[19] The social question during the war with France led to savage repression by ministers fearful of a domestic revolution. The agitation caused by the industrial expansion of the 1790's, and the high price of provisions, furnished enough combustible material to make the Addington cabinet immediately reopen negotiations for peace.

lain could not shake off his inherent distrust of the Soviet Union. As late as March, 1939, he admitted:

I must confess to the most profound distrust of Russia. I have no belief whatever in her ability to maintain an effective offensive, even if she wanted to. And I distrust her motives, which seem to me to have little connection with our ideas of liberty, and to be concerned only with getting every one else by the ears. [20]

Chamberlain was not alone in holding such views, but since he was prime minister it assured the disregard for Russia as a power which could be included in any possible combination against Germany.

It is doubtful whether Italy would ever have joined the "democracies" against Nazism, or that her military contribution could have been significant. After the fiasco of the Hoare-Laval pact and the sanctions imposed on her by the League of Nations, Italy moved steadily into the German camp. Once Mussolini had accepted the *Anschluss* in March, it was inconceivable that he could be enlisted against Hitler by September.

Japan could not be of much help to Britain in Europe, but Chamberlain foresaw by 1934 that a German-Japanese combination would pose a formidable threat to England. [21] He seems first to have thought that a "deal" with Japan might avoid a simultaneous confrontation in Europe and the Far East. This approach came to grief because of American opposition to concessions to Japan, and the effort was blocked by a pro-American group in London. Until 1937 Chamberlain thought that the Japanese challenge was negotiable and that Germany was the greater danger. "The latter is the problem to which we must now address ourselves." But in the calculations of the military planning staff the Japanese played a major role, especially since trouble in Europe encouraged them to take advantage of it in Asia. [22]

There still remained the United States and France. Relations with the former had been dominated by two issues during the interwar years: allied war debts and naval disarmament. Both were dead by 1938; no payments had been made to Washington since 1933, and naval rearmament had become essential. If Britain could take these steps on the grounds of necessity, the American response had invariably been one of morality. Thus, while official relations were cordial, Chamberlain despaired in private of any American support. He doubted that President Roosevelt was strong enough to over-

[20] Feiling, *op. cit.*, p. 403.

[21] *Ibid.*, p. 253.

[22] "If you want to understand Munich, you must look to Japan," declared Sir Horace Wilson, R. John Pritchard, "The Far East as an Influence on the Chamberlain Government's Pre-War European Policies," *Millennium*, II (1973–1974), pp. 7–23 (the Wilson quote is from p. 21).

come the outspoken isolationism (so evident after his "quarantine" speech), which circumscribed United States foreign policy. "It is always best and safest to count on nothing from the Americans but words," Chamberlain decided and excluded Washington from his considerations.[23] It was evident to one historian that

...the grim isolation of Britain must have been oppressive. The prim moralism of the United States must have distressed the Cabinet. President Roosevelt had recently described as one hundred per cent wrong the notion that the United States was lining up with Britain and France against Germany.[24]

Could France at least be depended on? Even a positive answer was not likely to offer much comfort to the British government. For France, allied to Czechoslovakia, would have to fight if Germany attacked the latter. Would she fulfill her obligations and how well prepared was France for war, were questions which the English ministers repeatedly asked themselves. Despite her "strong" army, Chamberlain thought she was "desperately weak in some vital spots," and he saw this as "a public danger just when she ought to be a source of strength and confidence..."[25] In short, the British doubted the only nation which stood by their side, and this skepticism was fully reciprocated. Given this atmosphere, it is hardly surprising that the English government avoided a policy which relied too much on its entente with France and sought alternatives elsewhere.

A note should be added here about the role of the empire in the formulation of appeasement. D. C. Watt and others have described in detail the opposition of the Commonwealth governments to a war over Czechoslovakia. The attempt to come to terms with Germany had the solid support of the Commonwealth prime ministers.[26] What has not been considered is how a growing concern for the empire's safety might motivate Great Britain to appease her opponents. The recent article by R. John Pritchard points strongly in that direction: the threat of Japan to the British position in the Far East could best be met by a settlement with Germany in Europe.[27] In 1801, Henry Dundas (if no one else in London) worried about the danger of a French attack on India by way of Egypt. Edward Ingram in a series of articles has examined the myths and realities of that affair.[28] The potential risk (after Abercromby's

---

[23] Feiling, *op. cit.*, p. 325.
[24] Robbins, *op. cit.*, p. 267.
[25] Feiling, *op. cit.*, pp. 323, 324 letter of January 16, 1938.
[26] Watt, *Personalities and Policies*, pp. 139–158, 159–174; Robbins, *op. cit.*, pp. 155–157.
[27] Pritchard, *op. cit.*, pp. 7–23.
[28] Edward Ingram, "The Defence of British India – I: The Invasion Scare of 1798," *Journal of Indian History*, 48 (1970), pp. 565–584; Edward Ingram, "A Preview of the Great Game in Asia –

victory it was no longer actual) made Hawkesbury insist that the French evacuate Egypt and this one condition remained unchanged in the entire peace negotiations. Each time protection for the empire was well worth the price of appeasement.

The appraisal of relative power, which necessarily precedes a policy of appeasement, faced similar circumstances in 1801 and 1938; in fact, the isolation of Great Britain was neither splendid nor even advisable. By being alone each time the position of Great Britain was untenable, yet she did not lose her nerve. Appeasement was hardly negotiating from strength, but neither Addington nor Chamberlain proved more accommodating than was necessary. Each man, in his own fashion, fought hard to obtain the best terms in a bad situation.

The specific motives for appeasement can be variously interpreted, but their role cannot be denied. Unfortunately, these do not tell the whole story. Another category, which might be called the uncertain motives, also exists. They are no less real, but it remains problematical to evaluate their influence. These uncertain motives are controversial, and have been equally asserted and denied. Still, such claims deserve examination.

What are we to think of fear as a motive? It is, after all, a legitimate emotion and a very human quality. It will not be difficult to prove that fear existed, though what its influence on policy may have been remains open to question. For our purposes it is possible to distinguish at least three types of fear: social and societal, ideological and military.

That fear about the prospects of her society existed in England during the years of the French revolution cannot be doubted. Even before the war with France began, in May 1792, the government issued a proclamation against seditious publications. With the war came hard times for the poor and a sharp increase in dissent. In 1794 the government sought to suppress opposition with a series of treason trials, but the defendants, who included the leaders of the London Corresponding Society, were freed of all charges. Discontent with the war, which was going badly, now burst into the open with public meetings in London; the King was shot at on the way to parliament, and on his return a mob surrounding his coach shouted: "Bread! Bread! Peace! Peace!"[29]

Appeals and petitions urged the Cabinet to end the fighting, and not only

---

III: The Origins of the British Expedition to Egypt in 1801," and "A Preview, etc., – IV: British Agents in the Near East in the War of the Second Coalition, 1798–1801," *Middle Eastern Studies*, IX (October, 1973), pp. 296–314, and X (January, 1974), pp. 15–35.

[29] S. Maccoby, *English Radicalism, 1786–1832: from Paine to Cobbett* (London, 1955), p. 94.

workers but businessmen and chambers of commerce sent such pleas.[30] Pitt countered this trend with repressive legislation: a Traitorous Correspondence Bill, the suspension of Habeas Corpus, and the Seditious Meetings Act. Enacted between 1794 and 1799, and renewed periodically thereafter, these laws deprived most Englishmen of their civil rights and by the end of the decade had succeeded in driving political agitation underground. Fox and his small group of Whigs, who had not joined the government, ceased attending parliament after 1798. But Pitt stood firm. "My head would be off in six months, were I to resign," he is reported to have said.[31]

This is not language designed to show confidence in the stability of English society. There has been much disagreement among historians whether England was in danger of a revolution, but these discussions have missed an important point. The question is not whether a revolution was about to take place, but what people *thought* might happen. Certainly, the naval mutinies of 1797, the many popular demonstrations and food riots, and the continued interest in the writings of Thomas Paine and similar works (which were being reprinted) were not of a nature to set political minds at rest.[32]

What made revolution in Britain such a distinct possibility, aside from the pressing domestic reasons, was the potent example across the Straits of Dover. Edmund Burke had early warned his countrymen about the nature of the revolution; you are in conflict with an "armed doctrine" he told them.[33] Pitt and his cabinet at first ignored Burke's ideological fears. But after repeated efforts to defeat France had ended in failure, and the Republic had shown no signs of being overcome financially, even the government had to admit the ideological factor. The survival of Jacobinism, in the words of Burke, would assure France as "a perpetual fund of revolution."[34] Belatedly, Pitt recognized the overwhelming danger of Jacobinism and revolution: "that torrent of liquid fire," as he called it.[35] Others had not been so slow, and one need only recall the antirevolutionary agitation and pamphleteering of John

---

[30] Jules Dechamps, *Les Iles britanniques et la Révolution française (1789–1803)* (Brussels, 1949), pp. 55–56.

[31] *The Life of William Wilberforce*, II, p. 114, November 16, 1795.

[32] Public meetings were of course illegal, unless the local authorities permitted them, and reprinting the words of Paine would land the printer in jail. Yet both happened during the 1790's. See e.g. Maccoby, *op. cit.*, p. 142.

[33] Carl B. Cone, *Burke and the Nature of Politics.* Vol. 2, *The Age of the French Revolution* (Lexington, Ky., 1964), p. 498.

[34] *Ibid.*, p. 421.

[35] *The War Speeches of William Pitt the Younger*, selected by R. Coupland, 3rd ed. (Oxford, 1940), p. 306.

Reeves, Hannah More, William Wilberforce and William Cobbett to grasp the magnitude of the ideological struggle.[36]

Whether these ideological and societal fears were justified remains in dispute till this day. Yet the confluence of war and lower class unrest, due in part to the industrial revolution, has been carefully analyzed.[37] Taken together these were worrisome conditions but by themselves not insuperable for the alert and rather efficient governing classes of the British isles. If another element is added, however, to the composite of motives – the fear of military invasion – the anxieties of cabinet and aristocracy become understandable.

Whether the invasion of England was militarily feasible is open to question, but it would have been folly to exclude the possibility. A small landing succeeded at Fishguard on the Welsh coast in 1797; there was also a measure of anxiety about the many French refugees in Britain, some of whom were suspected as a potential Fifth Column.[38] What might have happened if the invasion had succeeded? A hapless scholar, Gilbert Wakefield, published his opinion "that the labouring classes were so badly off that they could lose nothing by French conquest."[39] This was too much for the authorities, who feared exactly what Wakefield had dared to write, and he was put in prison for two years. That was in 1798, but three years later, on the very eve of the signing of peace preliminaries with France, Addington still worried about an invasion and complained to his brother that the newspapers treated the matter much too lightly.[40]

While it cannot be said with certainty that this compound of fears drove the Addington cabinet to make peace with Bonaparte "on any terms," the result of their agreement appears obvious.[41] It removed the immediate threat of invasion, while the restoration of peace eased conditions at home and freed the government's hands to deal with potential trouble spots. Thus, the end of

---

[36] M. G. Jones, *Hannah More* (Cambridge, 1952), p. 147 writes "It is probable that the Tracts [of Hannah More] did check disaffection and infidelity. The Prime Minister seemed to think so..."

[37] E. P. Thompson, *The Making of the English Working Class*, Vintage paperback ed. (New York, 1966), *passim*.

[38] For the landing at Fishguard, see E. H. S. Jones, *The Last Invasion of Britain* (Cardiff, 1950), *passim*. An interesting picture of the apprehension it caused in London can be found in a letter written nine days after the event, *The Journal of Mary Frampton, 1779–1846*, ed. by H. G. Mundy (London, 1885), pp. 93–94, Lady Elizabeth Talbot to Lady Harriet Fox Strangways, March 3, 1797.

[39] Francis E. Mineka, *The Dissidence of Dissent* (Chapel Hill, 1944), p. 24.

[40] See chapter II, footnote 18.

[41] The phrase quoted is from a contemporary newspaper article by William Cobbett, "To the Rt. Hon. Henry Addington," *Cobbett's Weekly Political Register*, March 20, 1802, p. 265.

the war quieted the fears about English society and the danger of revolution. It is true that a treaty with Bonaparte would confirm his usurpation and strengthen his government. But Bonaparte, it was widely believed, was the end of the revolution and so the end of Jacobinism.[42] Peace was well worth the price if it included the demise of ideological warfare.

Fear can be linked as well to the appeasement of the 1930's. It may not be possible to compare this uncertain motive in every instance, but the social, ideological and military components are easily identified. The social fears are least comparable, offering no actual but only potential concerns. Unlike the 1790's, when social fears were very real, British society during the 1930's was not suspected of teetering on the brink of revolution. Dissaffection there was, for the steady underemployment of the 1920's and the misery caused by the Depression had led individuals and groups beyond the point of mere dissent. The sympathetic interests of certain intellectuals for the Soviet system, the stalinism of Sir Stafford Cripps, or the naval mutiny at Invergordon were mere straws in the wind. Yet when unemployment assistance was cut in July, 1936, the author of this measure (Chancellor of the Exchequer Neville Chamberlain) foresaw that "the Communists may try to stage some disorder in South Wales."[43]

Often societal fears do not feed on the hard evidence of revolution, but on isolated incidents unrelated to trends. Despite economic recovery unemployment in 1937 stood at 1,600,000, and a National Unemployed Workers' Movement chose direct action as a means to dramatize their plight. Two hundred unemployed stopped traffic in Oxford Street by lying down; later,

---

[42] Pitt was quickly aware of the importance of Bonaparte's *coup d'état* on November 9, 1799. He sent a long memorandum which raised the question of a royal restoration, and of a peace offer, to General Charles Stuart. E. Stuart Wortley, *A Prime Minister and His Son: From the Correspondence of the 3rd Earl of Bute and of Lt.-General The Hon. Charles Stuart* (London, 1925), pp. 322–323, Mr. Pitt to Sir Charles Stuart, December 1, 1799. Cornwallis, in Ireland at this time, viewed Bonaparte's coup as tending "to discredit the plan of putting down established governments..." *Correspondence of Charles, First Marquis Cornwallis*, ed. by Charles Ross (London, 1859), III, p. 148, Cornwallis to Ross, November 29, 1799. "The cause of republicanism is over..." wrote Robert Southey to Samuel T. Coleridge on December 23, 1799. *New Letters of Robert Southey*, ed. by Kenneth Curry (New York, 1965), I, p. 211. George Canning, until March 1799 Under Secretary of Foreign Affairs, was jubilant about the change in France and sent letters to his friends, Lord Granville Leveson Gower and Lord Boringdon. Lord Granville Leveson Gower, *Private Correspondence, 1781–1821* (London, 1917), I, p. 273, Canning to Lord Gower, November 19, 1799; A. G. Stapleton, *George Canning and his times* (London, 1859), p. 43, "Buonaparte may flourish, but the idol of Jacobinism is no more." Canning to Lord Boringdon, November 19, 1799.

[43] Feiling, *op. cit.*, p. 287. In this connection, the General Strike of 1926 had made a profound impression on the leaders of the Conservative party. See Margaret George, *The Warped Vision. British Foreign Policy, 1933–1939* (Pittsburgh, 1965) p. 24.

one hundred invaded the Grill Room at the Ritz to ask for tea.[44] A stunt perhaps, but what did it foretell? A. J. P. Taylor has also pointed out that the limited recovery of the economy during the 1930's "...did not bring with it a softening of class antagonism. Rather there was a more aggressive tone of class war."[45]

It would have been easy to dismiss these tempests in English society if ideological factors had not been present. But once again, as in the earlier period, each social question had an ideological side even though similar fears were more complex. Not one but two ideologies – communism and nazism – assailed the ramparts of English life. Some Englishmen may have believed a choice between one or the other essential for survival; others thought that an accommodation with nazism would protect them from radical change. One evening in May, 1938 Harold Nicolson, on his way home, stopped off at Pratts' where he met three young peers. They told him "they would prefer to see Hitler in London than a Socialist administration." Sadly, Nicolson observed in his diary a few weeks later

People of the governing classes think only of their own fortunes, which means hatred of the Reds. This creates a perfectly artificial but at present most effective secret bond between ourselves and Hitler.[46]

How valid are these remarks? Nicolson was a clever observer but hardly a member of the "inner circle." Would ideological fears so affect the motivation for an understanding with Hitler? The conservative government of 1934, fearing communist propaganda in the armed forces, had restored the practice of general warrants which had not been used since the days of John Wilkes.[47] Chamberlain and the men around him had no use for fascism of any kind, but it appears that they regarded communism as a far greater *domestic* menace.

As an example, we have chosen of those who advised Chamberlain three who voiced their ideological fears: Lord Halifax, the Foreign Secretary, Sir Horace Wilson, Chief Industrial Adviser to the government and assigned for service with the Prime Minister, and Geoffrey Dawson, the editor of *The Times*. When Halifax met Hitler in November, 1937 he complimented the

[44] Robert Graves and Alan Hodge, *The Long Week-End. A Social History of Great Britain, 1918–1939.* Norton paperback ed. (New York, 1963), pp. 403–406.

[45] A. J. P. Taylor, *English History, 1914–1945. The Oxford History of England*, vol. 15 (Oxford, 1965), p. 346.

[46] Harold Nicolson, *Diaries and Letters, 1930–1939*, Vol. I (New York, 1966), pp. 342, 346, May 18, June 6, 1938. See also the comments of John A. Garraty, "The New Deal, National Socialism and the Great Depression," *American Historical Review*, 78 (October, 1973), pp. 936–938.

[47] Taylor, *English History*, p. 374; George, *op. cit.*, p. 22.

Führer for keeping communism out of Germany. In doing so, he had blocked its passage to the West.[48] In a few months' time Czechoslovakia seemed to be in danger of a German attack. During the May crisis the Foreign Secretary sent a personal message to the German Foreign Minister, Joachim von Ribbentrop. In case of a European conflagration, Halifax argued, "only those will benefit from such a catastrophe who wish to see destruction of European civilisation."[49]

On the eve of Munich Sir Horace Wilson had a conversation with the German chargé in London, Theodor Kordt. Sir Horace painted a very promising future for Germany, provided Hitler did not choose an aggressive course. Moreover,

It would be the height of folly if these two leading white races [England and Germany] were to exterminate each other in war. Bolshevism would be the only gainer thereby.[50]

The ideological concerns of Geoffrey Dawson have been admitted by his biographer. "Geoffrey was certainly influenced too by the thought that Nazi Germany served as a barrier to the spread of Communism in the West."[51] Of the three, Sir Horace was closest to Chamberlain on a daily basis, while Dawson appears to have been somewhat of an "idea man" for the Prime Minister.[52]

If ideological fears drove Englishmen to appease Hitler, uneasiness over military matters, and specifically war in the air, was a further inducement to meet Germany more than half way. Invasion in the traditional sense might be remote, but in the 1930's Great Britain was not safe from other "nations' airy navies grappling in the central blue." With the rearmament of Germany, and the creation of a modern air force, England faced an unprecedented challenge to her insular security. The Baldwin government was not unaware of this development or its dangers – thought it was hard to know precisely what was happening – but it met the problem in a rather confused way.

It is doubtful that any British minister has ever been more explicit about his

---

[48] Martin Gilbert, *The Roots of Appeasement* (New York, 1966), p. 162. Lord Cornwallis had paid Bonaparte a similar compliment when meeting him. He praised the First Consul for "having rescued his country from the confusion and anarchy [i.e., Jacobinism] by which it had been so long oppressed." *Cornwallis Correspondence*, III, p. 400. Marquis Cornwallis to Lord Hawkesbury, December 3, 1801.

[49] As quoted in Henri Noguères, *Munich. "Peace for Our Time"* (New York, 1965), p. 65. Henderson, unable to deliver Halifax's letter to Ribbentrop, spoke with State Secretary Ernst von Weizsäcker instead. Explaining its contents he added: "We should not let it [the May crisis] get out of hand, for then the only ones to profit would be the Communists." *Loc. cit.*

[50] As quoted in Northedge, *op. cit.*, pp. 519–520.

[51] John E. Wrench, *Geoffrey Dawson and Our Times* (London, 1955), pp. 362, 376.

[52] *Ibid.*, p. 375; Taylor, *English History*, p. 405; Watt, *Personalities and Policies*, pp. 12, 163.

military fears than Stanley Baldwin. At least he proceeded to scare both himself and "the man in the street" about the effects of aerial warfare and indiscriminate bombing. "Whatever people may tell him, the bomber will always get through."[53]

Playing upon his own fears, Baldwin pictured for his listeners – in the House of Commons – the horrors of attack from the air, cities in smoking ruins, millions of people dead or fleeing in panic of terror.[54]

But that was not all. "If London is bombed three nights running, nothing can avert a revolution."[55] That had been the warning of a socialist. No wonder Baldwin was certain that in the next war European civilization would be wiped out.[56]

In case it be thought that these words just represented one elderly minister's loss of nerve (which was true enough), the general mood in Britain about war and air power should not be overlooked. The pacifism of the 1935 Peace Ballot was reinforced by a dread about bombing, and because it was an unknown quantity this feeling was powerful. Baldwin's successor had none of his lethargy and prudence about rearmament or foreign affairs; Chamberlain sponsored a careful program which included re-equipping and modernizing the Royal Air Force. That this was meant to strengthen his hand in nego-tiation, rather than for making war, is now known. Neville Chamberlain abhorred war, and no clearer statement of his military fears can be found than in the diary of his Secretary of State for War. Hore-Belisha recorded a few days before the Munich conference:

The P.M. yesterday spoke to us of the horrors of war, of German bombers over London and of his horror in allowing our people to suffer all the miseries of war in our present state.[57]

When one scans the balance sheet of fear, whether for the 1790's or the 1930's, the totals are much the same: for all its uncertainty fear was strong enough to prompt English ministers into agreements which made undue concessions and held no assurance for future stability.

The record of uncertain motives for appeasement ought not to overlook two other human qualities: doubt and guilt. It is a matter of some interest that

---

[53] *House of Commons Debate*, Fifth Series, Vol. 270, p. 632.
[54] George, *op. cit.*, p. 51.
[55] G. M. Young, *Stanley Baldwin* (London, 1952), p. 174.
[56] *House of Commons Debate*, Fifth Series, Vol. 270, p. 638.
[57] As quoted in Iain Macleod, *Neville Chamberlain* (New York, 1962), p. 262. See also Feiling, *op. cit.*, p. 321.

while fear can be readily identified as a part of the ministerial outlook in both periods, doubt and guilt feelings are more prevalent among individual Englishmen. There was a large measure of doubt about the Addington and Chamberlain cabinets, a doubt about its competence to steer the country through the difficult times. Contemporary observations ranged from Canning's "Pitt is to Addington as London is to Paddington," or "the Pilot who moored us in Peace," to Churchill's comment that Chamberlain's view of world affairs was to look at it through a municipal drainpipe. Such cutting remarks hardly helped the government to strengthen its position *vis à vis* Bonaparte or Hitler, and the brunt of the political infighting may have softened it to the point of appeasement.

Doubt as a motive was more serious when it affected attitudes concerning war. The war weariness of 1801, the horror of war in 1938 reflected not just fear, but doubt about the usefulness of war as a policy. Pitt's several attempts to negotiate peace, as much as Addington's, and Chamberlain's journeys to Germany and Italy were vivid demonstrations that the British government questioned the wisdom of carrying out its policies with military means. This doubt was also enhanced by moral considerations; Pitt declared in 1797 that it was his duty as a Christian to end the war.[58] Chamberlain told the English people in a radio broadcast just before the Munich conference that he was "a man of peace to the depth of [his] soul. Armed conflict between nations is a nightmare to me..."[59]

Such doubts about the efficacy of war were not confined to ministers, however, but found a broad echo among most English men and women. After eight years of fighting, and no solution for the conditions in France at hand, war seemed no longer a sensible policy. There was no "benefit" to be had from the war, judged William Wilberforce; it was "like a bad habit of body."[60] "Blessed be the peacemakers," told Thomas Fremantle, a captain in the King's navy, to his wife.[61] "I am dying for peace," wrote Lady Sarah Napier Lennox from Dublin in April, 1801.[62] How many times must these sentiments among the upper classes have been repeated by the hungry and the poor of England?

That similar views about war existed during the 1930's is well known. The legacy of World War I – with its waste of human lives – was the strong

---

[58] J. Holland Rose, *William Pitt and the Great War* (London, 1911), p. 322.
[59] Feiling, *op. cit.*, p. 372.
[60] *Life of William Wilberforce*, III, pp. 10–11, July 30, 1801.
[61] *The Wynne Diaries*, ed. by Anne Fremantle, Vol. III, 1798–1820 (London, 1940), p. 30, Captain Thomas Fremantle to Elizabeth Wynne Fremantle, February 20, 1801.
[62] *The Life and Letters of Lady Sarah Lennox, 1745–1826*, ed. by the Countess of Ilchester and Lord Stavordale (London, 1901), I, p. 152.

conviction by many that it need not have taken place and that it had settled nothing. The rejection of war as a defensible policy for British statesmen is carefully summed up in a new study.[63] A further aspect of this scene was the rejection of the balance of power and the conclusion of alliances as a defensive measure. The practice of power politics was condemned as contributing much to the outbreak of war in 1914. The rejection of alliances in the 1930's bears an interesting comparison to Pitt's coalitions which repeatedly failed in their support of England's efforts. Whichever happened, the outcome was the same: Britain was left alone to face her continental adversary.

If doubt can be reckoned at least as an uncertain motive for appeasement, it cannot be understood without reference to "loss of nerve" as an English predicament. It may be impossible to document this state of mind; nevertheless, a number of signs point in this direction. The near-panic that seized Baldwin in speaking of bombing from the air, the fear of a lightening aerial descent on Britain, the hysteria in the House of Commons when Chamberlain announced the imminent Munich conference, the adulation which greeted him on his third return from Germany: here are but a few of the symptoms associated with this loss of nerve.[64] It would not be wise, however, to compare this condition with any similar state in the 1790's. There was no loss of nerve when Pitt resigned in 1801, although his resignation was partly the result of his inability to end the war. The panic of that *année terrible* – 1797 – had had no lasting effect, and though Britain was bone-tired of war and longed for peace, she had not lost her head.

Finally, there remains one other facet of doubt with its reflection on appeasement. In the 1790's Great Britain was an oligarchic society challenged by an egalitarian one, in the 1930's a political democracy nearly overcome by a depression and forced to deal with a dictatorship which seemingly had put its economic house in order. These are oversimplifications, of course, but each attempts to make this point: while British society experienced much difficulty, its adversary seemed to offer a better life to its citizens. The attractions of the "organized society" made few converts in the twentieth century, while the egalitarianism of revolutionary France was too stained with blood to gain a large following in England. Still, these new social models created doubts about the British way of life which functioned only imperfectly. How widespread or influential this feeling was it would be hard to say, but one may venture to think that such doubts about one's own society helped to smooth the path of appeasement.

[63] Keith Robbins, *Munich, 1938*, especially pp. 14–46, 123–132.
[64] George, *The Warped Vision, passim*, reviews this loss of nerve among the Conservative leadership in great detail.

Guilt feelings are certainly as strong as doubt and perhaps more influential. In the spectrum of motives guilt has a clearly identifiable tint. It proved to be a powerful inducement to appeasement in Germany's case. The cause of this stance was the treaty of Versailles. There was some thought that the indictment should cover the general election of 1918 as well, for it had stirred up the fearful anti-German attitudes which were incorporated in the peace treaty. Opinion was certainly not unanimous on the subject, and as long as the Weimar republic projected an image of helplessness, those in power in Great Britain were not inclined to allow their consciences to dictate policy.

Until 1933, therefore, a measure of guilt about the treatment of Germany would have been acknowledged by many Englishmen, but few were ready to do more. Hitler and the revival of German strength changed all that. For those who had always regretted the peace treaty, the "new" Germany represented a final chance to overcome the injustices of yesterday. Others not so sensitive to history were inclined to agree now that nazism was in power.[65] The sense of guilt affected especially persons with strong religious convictions; Lord Lothian and Robert Barrington-Ward may be mentioned as examples. The first, a former Roman Catholic turned Christian Scientist, visited Hitler three times. An ardent appeaser, Lothian believed that "Nazi brutality was largely the reflex of the external persecution to which Germans had been subjected since the war."[66] Lothian had ready access to Chamberlain, and delivered a personal report after returning from Germany.

Few people declared their sense of guilt in more explicit terms than Robert Barrington-Ward, the chief assistant to the editor of *The Times*, and subsequently the editor himself. Barrington-Ward knew German and had read *die Grosse Politik*, but he gave full support to Dawson's pro-German attitude and editorials in *The Times*. In the words of *The Times*' history,

In principle, B.-W. accepted the German thesis that the Treaty was unjust, and he had believed ever since Versailles that the Anschluss was inevitable and should have been conceded to Brüning. Having come to this conclusion before Hitler was ever heard of, he could see no reason in conscience for refusing justice to Germany after Hitler was in power...[67]

Because his opinions were based on the "moral decision" he had made about the peace treaty, Barrington-Ward could write: "...we are, as the Prayer

[65] Watt, *Personalities and Policies*, pp. 117–135.
[66] As quoted in Christopher Thorne, *The Approach of War, 1938–1939* (New York, 1968), p. 16.
[67] *The History of The Times, 1921–1948* (London, 1952), p. 913. Franklin R. Gannon, *The British Press and Germany, 1936–1939* (Oxford, 1971), p. 63.

Book says, tied and bound by the chains of our sins stretching all the way back to the General Election of 1918."[68]

Is there any point of comparison between this tendency and the urge for peace with revolutionary France? Comparative history is not an exercise in exactitude, but even so delicate a subject as guilt may have precedents. At least one person – Charles Fox – voiced his concern about the treatment revolutionary France had received at the hands of England and her allies. It is doubtful that he was alone; Coleridge's friend and man of affairs Thomas Poole expressed his sympathy for the French side.[69] Fox, however, went further than anyone else, and remained consistent about it. He had embraced the French revolution with warm feeling, calling the fall of the Bastille "the greatest event ... that ever happened in the world! and how much the best."[70]

From the outbreak of the war, which he denounced, till the restoration of peace, he kept up a steady criticism of Pitt and the conflict with France. Fox did not condemn the war for its own sake, but because he held that France had the better cause. It did not matter that his party deserted him, that the divisions in the lobby overwhelmed him, and that for three years he absented himself from the House of Commons because there was nothing else he could do to indicate his dissent. When peace was restored he praised it as glorious to France without bothering to hide the contempt he felt for his own government. "The triumph of the French government over the English does in fact afford me a degree of pleasure which it is very difficult to disguise." And somewhat later, at a meeting, he declared:

The peace is glorious to France-glorious to the First Consul. Ought it not to be so? Ought not glory to be the reward of such a glorious struggle? France has set an example that will be highly useful to all the nations of the earth, and above all to Great Britain.[71]

Perhaps Barrington-Ward's confused morality and Fox's obstinate sympathy cannot be compared. What was a sense of guilt in one amounted to a spirit of humanity in the other. And yet a similar rule – that of fair play – motivated them both. The war against France outraged Fox, the peace with

[68] *History of The Times*, pp. 901, 913.
[69] Mrs. Henry Sandford, *Thomas Poole and his friends* (London, 1888), I, pp. 164, 221–222, II, p. 4. Even the commander of the British troops during their unsuccessful expedition to Holland in 1799 expressed an unusual appreciation for the French. They were "perfectly civilized," wrote Sir Ralph Abercromby to his family, October 31, 1799. *Lieutenant-General Sir Ralph Abercromby K.B., 1793–1801*. A memoir by his son James, Lord Dunferline (Edinburgh, 1861), p. 201.
[70] Christopher Hobhouse, *Fox* (London, 1947), p. 188.
[71] *Ibid.*, p. 235. The first quote is from a letter to Charles Grey of October 22, 1801.

Germany offended Barrington-Ward. In each a sense of decency was injured to the point where subsequent appeasement seemed the only policy to right a previous wrong. It is not too much to say that each man, though without real influence, had enough of a following to project his feelings, to create an atmosphere. Since appeasement was in the air, a full consideration of the subject could not ignore their uncertain contribution.

Finally, our discussion of motives should consider appeasement as a personal expression, the tangible form of an inner drive. Appeasement as the self realization of this or that politician may appear ridiculous. Still, persons have testified how much Chamberlain accepted appeasement as a mission, or how urgently Addington had declared his intention to negotiate peace with Bonaparte.[72] Thus, the personality of a prime minister – the projection of the self – can become a motive for appeasement.

Much has been written about the role of the individual in history; to focus on the personality of a prime minister as a motive for appeasement may be construed as an endorsement of that approach. It is indeed difficult to conceive the Munich conference without Neville Chamberlain, or the treaty of Amiens without Henry Addington. Pitt would not sign a peace which granted France much and England little, and guaranteed that little badly. Nor would Stanley Baldwin seek Hitler out and fly three times to Germany. As a matter of fact, we know that he avoided meeting Hitler, although pressured to do so by his confidant Tom Jones.[73] Addington's naïveté and complacency contrast sharply with Pitt's calculating sense of what was owing to him. Similarly, Chamberlain's directness and conceit was a clear break from Baldwin's lassitude and lack of involvement.

That the personality of a prime minister might contain a motive for appeasement emphasizes the importance of the office. It does not endorse the doctrine that persons rather than ideas or movements make history. There are, after all, many motives for appeasement, of which personality is but the last and not necessarily the least influential.

* * *

[72] Thorne, *op. cit.*, p. 20, in referring to Chamberlain, states "Appeasement became a mission..." Feiling, *op. cit.*, p. 365 called Chamberlain's policies "an act of faith." Addington told the American minister in London that "neither success nor adversity would change their wishes" for peace. It is strange that he would express himself so categorically to a minor diplomat. *The Life and Correspondence of Rufus King*, ed. by Charles R. King (New York, 1896), III, p. 443, May 6, 1801. See also Malmesbury, *op. cit.*, IV, p. 29, March 4, 1801, "Addington's mind is full of peace..."

[73] Although Pitt may have advised and supported Addington in the negotiations with France, he bore no responsibility for the treaty, and many thought at the time that he had deliberately done so. On Baldwin's reluctance to see Hitler, see Tom Jones, *A Diary with Letters, 1931–1950* (London, 1954), pp. 194–205.

This study attempts not only to analyze appeasement, but to do it on a comparative basis. How valid, however, are our comparative assumptions? Obviously the role and importance of similarity is central to this question. For this purpose we are using the dictionary definition of similarity: "nearly but not exactly the same or alike." In order to achieve meaningful comparisons three categories of similarities will be presented: major similarities, minor ones and odd similarities.

It is possible to disagree with this categorization as too contrived, but it will be harder to challenge the process by which historical events are related in terms of similarity to earlier historical occurrences. Unless one believes each historical event to be unique, it is logical to attempt explanation by way of comparison.[74] There can be no comparing in history without some similarity, and without comparison historical explanation is reduced to the task of interpreting autonomous incidents.

The description of the individual event is history, and a readily accepted form of history at that. Yet it is not always the most satisfactory form of history, especially when historians seek to achieve a more incisive understanding from broad perspectives. General conclusions can be drawn when historical events are put to the test of comparison, and such conclusions will have greater validity if the comparison is based on similar experiences.

Among the major similarities to be considered first is the challenge to England's existence which developed on the European continent in the 1790's and the 1930's. At least it was viewed as a challenge in London. Though she responded more rapidly in the earlier period than in the more recent one, the basis of her reaction was the same. As an island she has always been sensitive to movements or conditions which may lead to the unification of Europe. Separated from the continent in many ways, England fears a united Europe as tantamount to an invasion of her shores. This is especially true when such unification might be achieved through military means. The history of Europe has amply justified these fears.

The broad similarity of military circumstances notwithstanding, there are enough differences to take a closer look. The war between France and the German states (Austria and Prussia) did not touch England at first. But in October, 1792, the French troops entered what is now Belgium. In the course of its advance the revolutionary army broke a number of international agreements to which Great Britain was a party. The most serious of these was the reopening of the Scheldt estuary and the port of Antwerp to international

---

[74] It might be pointed out that in law the concept of precedent is largely based on comparisons.

trade. Now England was involved, or soon would be since there was evidence of French intentions regarding Holland and the Dutch were allied to Great Britain.

All this is too well known to be retold. What is important is the character of the war and its growing challenge to Great Britain. French ambitions in Europe were not new, nor was England's concern about the status of the Low Countries and who controlled the coast of Flanders. She chose to fight France in order to defend her Dutch ally, but soon much more was at stake. The French won the battles and the English, defeated, withdrew. This did not end the war, for England subsidized her allies to keep on fighting. As the war went on and widened in scope the French faced new enemies. Russia and Naples joined the struggle while Prussia withdrew. All of Europe was now a battlefield and France seemed to be winning. England, which had entered the war to secure the Dutch coast, found herself fighting for her life against a France which nearly dominated the continent.

On the surface the circumstances of the 1930's were rather different. Britain was much slower to face the challenge from Germany or to prepare her response. But she did not fail to act from lack of experience. Only twenty years before Germany had tried through military means to achieve hegemony in Europe. It was hard to imagine she would ever attempt anything like that again. Thus, Germany's outspoken policies during the 1930's were regarded initially as only complaints about an unsatisfactory peace settlement. If the danger from Nazi Germany seemed small at first, by 1938 it had become unmistakable. This was not because of ideology or aggressive plans, though these factors are not to be discounted, but rather that any war involving Germany would soon engulf the entire continent. Here was the core of England's concern. Unless Germany could be defeated in short order, which was highly unlikely, her conflict with any state might end with Europe being ruled from Berlin.

The variation in our similarity of military circumstances is now clear. In 1793, Great Britain went to war against France only dimly aware of the challenge; in 1939 she declared war because she had no other choice and was all too well aware what a German victory would mean. In either case failure to meet the challenge would have meant the end of her independent national existence.

A similarity of dangers might be a coincidence, but this seems unlikely since it was not just a military matter but an ideological confrontation as well. The ideological factor strengthened the military challenge and was at times viewed in England with greater alarm than a physical invasion by enemy soldiers. This was certainly true in the earlier period when "French ideas" were denouced as alien to the British way of life. The ideological conditions of the 1930's were more complicated since not one but two doctrinal systems competed with each other and the English political style.

In British eyes the egalitarianism of the French revolution was an ideological thrust directed against all social and political systems. The Cabinet watched with rising concern the humiliation and trial of Louis XVI, the cooperation between General Dumouriez and certain Belgian democratic circles, and the appearance of new political clubs at home, of which the London Corresponding Society was the most prominent. Conspiracy seemed in the air, at least to the suspicious mind, which also found much support for its views in the publications of Edmund Burke. If additional evidence were needed that an ideological offensive was being conducted from Paris, the National Convention passed the First Propaganda Decree on November 19, 1792. It promised assistance and friendship to all peoples who wished to throw off their government.

There are suggestions that the decree was not at all a call for international revolution, but an effort to protect Belgian and Rhineland democrats, who were helping French troops, from counterrevolutionary reprisals. The French foreign ministry even informed neutral states (England and Switzerland) that they were excluded from the scope of the proclamation.[75] But the British government chose not to interpret it that way. Within eight days of this decree the French opened the Scheldt to commerce and to all intents and purposes England ceased to be a neutral. Perhaps the First Propaganda Decree was only political *braggadocio*, but contemporaries did not view it in that light. In the opinion of one Englishman writing to his brother, the Foreign Secretary

...the infection is gaining ground in every quarter, and it is a painful reflexion for us to know that there is not in this country a military force which can effectually check the first burst of the fire, if it should catch here with the same rapidity with which it spreads in other parts of Europe.[76]

Did a similar ideological challenge confront England during the 1930's? Undoubtedly yes, provided certain details are taken into consideration.

[75] Steven T. Ross, *European Diplomatic History, 1789–1815: France against Europe* (New York, 1969), pp. 60–62; Bryant, *Years of Endurance*, pp. 98–99.

[76] Historical Manuscripts Commission, *The Manuscripts of J. B. Fortescue, Esq., preserved at Dropmore*, Vol. II (London, 1894), p. 327, The Marquis of Buckingham to Lord Grenville, November 8, 1792. The day France declared war on Britain (February 1, 1793), Pitt told the House of Commons: "They [i.e., the French] will not accept, under the name of liberty, any model of government but that which is conformable to their own opinions and ideas... They have stated that they would organise every country by a disorganising principle..." As quoted in Bryant, *Years of Endurance*, p. 105.

Hitler and Mussolini talked constantly of fascist and authoritarian strengths as compared with democratic weaknesses. The dynamic qualities of their regimes would prove superior to the tired and anemic system of the liberal states. The full-employment economy of Germany (though not Italy) was the envy of the depression-racked democracies, but neither Englishmen nor Frenchmen found much appeal in the ideological structure that accompanied this achievement.

Still, the depression spelled danger as long as it persisted. Could democracy survive alongside mass unemployment? In Germany it had not, but even if the siren call of fascism attracted very few in England she was not out of danger. The example of the Spanish civil war served as a warning what might happen if a nation became wholly polarized. The late Victorians who governed England suspected that "the social question" would promote the chances for other ideologies like communism. The challenge was not in the possible acceptance of communism by the English working class – a rather unlikely suggestion. The danger, as Baldwin and others sensed it, was the conflict arising from the chance to divide along doctrinal lines.[77] Not only were communism and fascism "un-British" – foreign imports – but they arrived at a time of severe economic distress. Even England's democracy might not be able to stand the strain of ideological challenge and conflict in the midst of a depression.

The ideological problem also affected Baldwin and Chamberlain in different ways. It almost paralyzed the first; he avoided meeting Hitler and eventually shied away from foreign affairs altogether. His time and energy were absorbed in managing democracy, although he might talk occasionally about "limit [ing] the franchise."[78] Chamberlain, less subtle than Baldwin, suspected communism but viewed the nazi threat only in terms of power. By downgrading nazi ideas, and dealing with its regime in the hope of avoiding war, he seemed to be taking sides. We know he did not, but so it appeared. The effect was to aggravate the ideological divisions.

The similarity of military and ideological challenge met an analogous response in each period with the crusade for peace. If it is understood that the peace drive peaked both times in the intermission between two wars, the similar nature of this movement becomes clear. No sooner had war been declared in 1793, than Fox in parliament and dissent outside it called for peace. By 1795 Pitt came to consider negotiating with France, and the urge for peace received new support. Now Wilberforce added his voice in the House of

77 Northedge, *op. cit.*, pp. 385–386.
78 George, *op. cit.*, p. 44.

Commons while workingmen's clubs and merchant associations petitioned the King to dismiss his ministers and sue for terms. "Never was there a war carried on with such an incessant cry for peace from the very beginning of it." Windham, who spoke these words during the debate on the peace treaty with France, regretted that the "public mind" had gotten its way.[79]

The war with France resumed in May, 1803. It was a new struggle and most Englishmen acknowledged that it had to be fought. The peace movement had run its course; the war with France, now ruled by Bonaparte, was different from the earlier conflict with the French republic. In the 20th century this pattern of war, strong peace drive and war once more would be repeated, though over a longer span of time. The first war with Germany saw relatively little agitation for peace so long as the fighting continued. During the 1920's, and especially in the thirties, the peace movement gathered much strength. In the earlier phase it promoted disarmament; after 1934 it managed to delay the rearmament of England and France. With the renewal of war in 1939, the peace efforts ceased as Englishmen accepted once more the necessity of fighting. The quest for peace had failed. Neither the phenomenon nor the outcome were unique. Only the sequence of events was remarkable in its resemblance.

The challenges confronting England constitute one kind of major similarity. However, conditions in Europe as these were watched and interpreted in London, offer another important parallel. The appearance of ceasarism in 1799 and 1933 was quickly noted by the English government. For Windham the consulate was a government "dropt from the clouds, or rather starting from underneath the ground..."[80] Both he and Canning were resolutely against negotiations with Bonaparte, as was of course Grenville, the Foreign Secretary. Pitt seemed uncertain what the change in France meant, and apparently considered the possibility of negotiating before Bonaparte made any overtures.[81] So, too, there was concern about Hitler before he even attained office; in 1931 Neville Chamberlain accused the French of promoting his "advent ... to power" by being inflexible on reparations.[82] After the Nazis had taken over, Sir Horace Rumbold, the British ambassador in Berlin, warned his government about "these gangsters" and predicted that they

---

[79] *Parliamentary History of England*, XXXVI, p. 750, May 13, 1802.

[80] *The Windham Papers*, with an introduction by the Rt. Hon. the Earl of Roseberry (Boston, 1913), II, p. 143, William Windham to William Pitt, November 18, 1799.

[81] See Pitt's letter of December 1, 1799, with Enclosure, to Sir Charles Stuart, in Wortley, *op. cit.*, pp. 322–323.

[82] Feiling, *op. cit.*, p. 201, December 6, 1931.

would rearm Germany. One of his dispatches (April 26, 1933) was circulated to the entire Cabinet to read.[83]

Yet were Bonaparte and Hitler so alike that they can be mentioned in the same breath? From the perspective of London they no doubt were. Both tried to rule the European continent, and leaving all other historical circumstances aside, their efforts assured them the hostility of England. Churchill understood this when he told the foreign affairs committee of the House of Commons in 1936 that any policy which surrendered eastern Europe to Germany would make her "dominant from Hamburg to the Black Sea, and we should be faced by a confederacy such as had never been seen since Napoleon."[84] But this was a voice in the wilderness.

At first the role of either seemed restricted to his own country. Bonaparte concluded peace with Austria (Russia had left the war); Hitler set about to restore Germany to economic health. Domestic reforms occupied most of their time in these early years. In foreign affairs neither Bonaparte in 1801, nor Hitler in 1938, had gone so far that agreement with them appeared impossible. There was of course evidence that each had larger goals, but the English government in both cases did not regard it as conclusive and chose to negotiate a settlement. After another year each dictator crossed the threshold to enter the era of his greater ambitions. The principles that had protected the revolutionary gains and natural frontiers of France, and the right of self determination for all Germans, ceased to guide policy while naked conquest and forced annexation became the order of the day. As Bonaparte and Hitler quit being "reasonable," England abandoned conciliation and became an implacable foe. Both leaders responded the same way by mobilizing every anti-English sentiment on the continent against her. Major historical differences between them remain, but their relations with England and her reactions in peace and war are striking in their similarity.

Another significant analogy can be drawn between the revolutionary decades of the 1790's and the 1930's. The upheavals of Europe affected English domestic affairs, which were already having problems, by influencing public opinion unfavorably about the existing political organizations. Pitt's government, at war abroad, reacted to dissent at home with repressive legislation. Baldwin and Chamberlain faced a more complex problem: how to provide the means for British security in the midst of a depression. They were caught between dangers abroad, which they did not fully comprehend, and the

---

[83] *The Diplomats, 1919–1939*, ed. by Gordon A. Craig and Felix Gilbert (New York, Atheneum paperback, 1963), II, pp. 445–447; Martin Gilbert and Richard Gott, *The Appeasers* (Cambridge, 1963), pp. 12–13.

[84] Nicholson, *Diaries and Letters*, I, p. 269, July 16, 1936.

chance of defeat at the polls at home, which they understood all too well. Fundamentally, each time the Cabinet was caught between simultaneous perils in foreign and domestic affairs, and it attempted to escape by negotiating a solution abroad.

The impact of the French revolution on public opinion and political parties in England was profound. Initially, there was a large measure of curiosity and support for events in France. But the press and reading public changed its attitude as the revolution grew more extreme by 1792. There followed an upsurge of loyalist sentiment for king and country; never before had George III been so popular with his own subjects. Within the narrower confines of British politics the effects of the French revolution were even more astonishing. One of the major political groups – the Whigs – under the stress of hatred and sympathy for the events in France split into irreconcilable parts. Burke and the nominal leader of the Whigs, the Duke of Portland, lent their support to Pitt who in 1794 formed a coalition cabinet. Fox and his small circle of friends remained in opposition.[85] Events abroad had given Pitt an overwhelming strength in the House of Commons, but what the Foxites lacked in numbers they made up by their outspoken opposition to the war and their endorsement of the changes in France.

The triumph of the Nazi movement in Germany found Great Britain still distracted by the crisis of 1931. There was no widespread support for the Nazi example as a solution to England's ills, although the noisy but small Mosley movement must be mentioned. One cannot even speak of an outburst of sympathy or encouragement as for the French revolution; indeed, the persecution of the Jews and the purge of 1934 produced quite the opposite effect. Gradually, however, some of this antipathy dissolved as the new regime regimented Germany. The end of unemployment by 1935 contrasted sharply with conditions in England where the number of unemployed two years later still stood at 1,376,000.[86]

Many English travellers commented favorably on the orderly conditions in Germany's cities, and the apparent elimination of "loose living and entertainment" which had been so evident during the Weimar republic. The dynamism, the vibrant energy of the Germans was being channeled into constructive projects compared to Great Britain, where neither the government nor the economic system seemed capable of providing a solution. These superficial comments and observations were enhanced by the rabid anticommunism of the Nazis, an orientation which did them no harm in the

---

[85] F. O'Gorman, *The Whig Party and the French Revolution* (New York, 1967), *passim*.
[86] W. H. Richardson, *Economic Recovery in Britain, 1932–1939* (London, 1967), p. 22. The largest number of unemployed existed in 1933, when 2,845,000 were out of work.

propaganda war. In a narrow circle of English conservatives open admiration for the Nazi regime was much in evidence, but among the larger share of the reading public awe for Germany's recovery was mixed with doubts about the ultimate consequences of the regime.

There is one important difference in this analysis. The small band of Foxites were highly vocal, and they might maintain social friendships with former Whigs or Tories, but they were essentially without influence. Their continued endorsement of "French principles" stripped their dissent of respectability. This was not the case during the 1930's when persons like Lord Lothian or Geoffrey Dawson, who looked with favor on Nazi Germany, had constant access to those in power, but in expressing admiration for Hitler's regime did not condemn themselves to oblivion.

If either French or Nazi revolution had taken place at a time when Great Britain was free from domestic unrest she might have responded very differently. In the 1790's, however, her industrial growth spawned social and economic problems, while the war with France caused much hardship with the sharp rise in food prices. The development of industry brought many people into the towns which could hardly hold them, while simultaneously on the land there was a concerted effort to reduce the population and enclose the farms. The political unrest arising from these conditions is well known, and drew its inspiration from many different sources. Mass meetings led to demands for Pitt's resignation and an end to the war.[87] Political protest in the 1790's had the support of journeymen and merchants, city workers and tenant farmers, all of whom had been hurt by the combination of war and the new ways of production. As the demands intensified, they focused on reform of the House of Commons to make it a more representative body. By itself this goal was not new, and in the 1780's it had received the cautious support of Pitt.

The decade of war, revolution and jacobinism defeated the renewed agitation for changes in representation. The cabinet was unwilling, or unable, to see that the movement for reform had English roots, and chose to act as if a foreign-inspired conspiracy was on foot. It fought back with treason trials and repressive legislation until the agitation was reduced to silence. Although ministers were successful on the political level, the government did not overcome the economic hardships and the consequent unrest. In 1801, when Addington succeeded Pitt, the country was still plagued by food riots and high prices from one end to the other. Moreover, the cabinet's policies invited

---

[87] See e.g. S. Maccoby, *English Radicalism, 1786–1832*, *passim*, and E. P. Thompson, *The Making of the English Working Class*, *passim*.

several financial disasters. At the start of the war in 1793 many country banks failed, but worse was to come in 1797. The export of gold subsidies to Great Britain's allies led to a run on the Bank of England. Only the suspension of payments in gold, and the imposition of new and onerous taxes made it possible to carry on the war. Until then Pitt had been reluctant to spend enough for Britain to fight effectively, or to mobilize the economy. His talents had restored England's economic health after the American war and now he resisted the costs of defending it.

The issues which disturbed England's domestic affairs during the thirties were unemployment and the slow pace of her economic recovery. Unemployment had plagued British life since 1919; although the depression had made it worse the lack of work was already a familiar affliction. This did not lessen the bitterness and despair which came with the growing inability to find employment. Even though the government refused to sponsor public works, there was remarkably little social tension. A construction boom in the mid-thirties provided new jobs for those capable of doing the work. Much dissatisfaction arose from the lack of an official program, but the fiscal orthodoxy of Neville Chamberlain and Sir John Simon, Chancellor of the Exchequer from 1937, inhibited a full-employment budget. Ministers were not unaware of the discontent caused by the unemployment of thousands, yet they remained anchored to the belief that recovery was dependent on demand catching up with supply.

If England saw little overt unrest during the depression, the potential for trouble loomed large in the minds of the policy makers in Whitehall and Downing Street. Who could be certain that the occasional strike would not blossom into a general one like 1926? That event had made a searing impression on the minds of leading Conservative politicians.[88] The government was not worried that the ideology of the right (Sir Oswald Mosley) or of the left (Marxist intellectuals and mavericks like Sir Stafford Cripps) might capture the will of the working class. But it feared the effects of its own policies, especially rearmament. Aside from pacifist or pro-German sympathies, the expenditures for rearmament would be resented in light of the government's unwillingness to sponsor public works projects. There might be no revolution, but to Baldwin the rejection of his policies at the polls would have been just as bad.

Since rearmament was necessary, but could not be acknowledged for a variety of reasons, it was implemented in a minor key. Nothing was done which might disturb the pound or economic recovery. To have done so could

---

[88] For Baldwin, see Northedge, *op. cit.*, p. 385; for Chamberlain, Feiling, *op. cit.*, p. 157.

have set off domestic repercussions. One is reminded here of Pitt's reluctance to mobilize the economy for the war with France, though Chamberlain and Sir Warren Fisher, the permanent Under Secretary of the Treasury, thought in terms of defense rather than war.[89] Chamberlain resented the waste of war and the costs of arming Britain, but Baldwin could only think of the political consequences. Domestic conditions could hardly have tied ministers' hands more without an open demonstration of discontent.

Finally, the treaty of Amiens and the Munich agreement should be considered under the rubric of major similarities. At first glance this seems barely possible, for Amiens was a peace treaty and Munich a diplomatic agreement. Moreover, the treaty covered the globe while the agreement truncated a single country. While this is true, a closer analysis will remove most of these objections. Four powers – France, Germany, Great Britain and Italy – signed the Munich document. Similarly, four states – France, Great Britain, Holland and Spain – put their signatures on the peace of Amiens. Yet each time the understanding was really between Great Britain and one antagonist, be it France or Germany. The other co-signers were only secondary participants.

More important, the Munich agreement underwrote Hitler's power in central and southeastern Europe. Did the Amiens treaty provide less for Bonaparte's influence in continental affairs? It is true that the peace treaty also dealt with colonial matters, but except for Ceylon and Trinidad, Britain retained none of her conquests. A large part of the treaty was devoted to the Isle of Malta. In omitting any reference to the independence of Holland, Belgium, Switzerland or northern Italy, the English government lost the opportunity to control the extension of French power.[90] In other words, the treaty of Amiens greatly enhanced the French position in Europe. The agreement at Munich accomplished the same for Germany. Both documents affected Europe much more than the overseas territories where England gained little and France returned to her pre-war status. But the French colonies were never very safe as long as the British fleet controlled the oceans.

One other point is to be made. At Amiens, as at Munich, Great Britain obtained the peace she wanted so badly. Each time she paid for it with the territory of smaller states. The English lost nothing – except prestige. But did this matter, did the English people care about an intangible loss? Those who

---

[89] Feiling, *op. cit.*, p. 314; Watt, *Personalities and Policies*, pp. 100–116. A. J. P. Taylor, *The Origins of the Second World War*, Fawcett paperback (New York, 1961), pp. 116–117.

[90] The treaty of Lunéville between France and Austria had provided for the independence of these states. Although England had not signed the treaty, she thought she could rely on its provisions. When Bonaparte violated its clauses, and England protested, he refused to recognize her protests since she was not a party to the agreement.

raised their voices against the settlements, Grenville and Windham (who was called Burke's ghost), Churchill and Duff Cooper, were rejected as extremists. Peace was reasonable, middle of the road and the public wanted no more heroics. Ultimately, Amiens and Munich have this in common: on the English side both settlements were the handiwork of moderate men in an immoderate age.

There are, to be sure, other historical similarities, but they are less central to appeasement. Although interesting to relate, such instances must be seen from a lower perspective. The two prime ministers, the appeal of appeasement, the passive and active stages of appeasement, the frustrations with the settlement: each of these subjects offers some similarity in a historical context.

What do Addington and Chamberlain have in common? Far more than one would first suspect. Both were of middle class origin: Addington was the son of a doctor while Chamberlain came from a business family. Neither was judged to be a future prime minister when he first entered parliament. Addington and Chamberlain were men of limited means and intelligence. A recent estimate of Addington might fit Chamberlain very well.

As a Minister, above all as Prime Minister, his deficiencies were obvious. He lacked imagination and a broad grasp of policy; he lacked flexibility; he lacked enterprise; above all he lacked grandeur and the art of kindling enthusiasm in the public. But he had qualities too. He was determined; he was courageous; he was thorough; he was indomitable in the defence of what he believed to be right ... Given a job to do, clearly defined and soluble by conventional techniques, Sidmouth would see it through against all difficulties and opposition. Only in the uncharted fields of wider policy did he begin to founder...[91]

If Addington was "dull," Chamberlain competed by being "humdrum." The former had reached his high office by accident or luck perhaps, the latter through endurance and party service. Neither had in fact a modest opinion of his talents. Though contemporaries ridiculed their abilities, each was convinced that such criticism was unfair.[92] Both were prime minister for three years, and both resigned when their large majority in the House of Commons was pared drastically by abstention or defection of the party faithful. There was much of the same in the quality of their leadership: a devotion to routine and established practices, a lack of oratorical skill, an overdependence on large majorities in the House to pass measures which failed to excite en-

[91] Ziegler, *Addington ... First Viscount Sidmouth*, pp. 421–422.
[92] According to Pitt, Addington was "a man of little mind, of consummate vanity and of very slender abilities." Rose, *William Pitt and the Great War*, p. 477. "There are some who think I [Chamberlain] am over-cautious, – timid, Amery calls it – humdrum, commonplace, and unenterprising. But I know that charge is groundless...," Feiling, *op. cit.*, p. 235.

thusiasm. And each loved power that he fought hard to retain it, perhaps against the better instincts of the party leaders. Addington, standing forever in the shadow of Pitt, repeatedly tried to bring him into the existing cabinet but would not make way for him. After Munich Chamberlain wanted "a few more years" before "he would go with an easy mind."[93]

The poor reputation of appeasement since World War II tends to obscure the appeal it once had. Its popularity was widespread, it cut across traditional lines and its was not the exclusive policy of any interest group. In short, appeasement was no upper class phenomenon. Beyond the general un-popularity of war in 1795 or 1938, certain circles were particularly vocal in dissent and in their subsequent endorsement of a peace policy.

The war with France found no support among such intellectuals as Sou-they, Coleridge, Wordsworth or Blake. Perhaps their stance must be seen in ideological terms, for all voiced some sympathies with "French ideas" at one time or other. It was not easy to come to terms with the French republic, and some of those who had condemned the war were equally unhappy with the peace. Coleridge considered it disgraceful. Businessmen like Thomas Poole were even more outspoken in their disagreement with the government's policies. Some business communities petitioned for peace while anti-slavery proponents like Wilberforce introduced motions against the war in the House of Commons. Finally, defeatists like Cornwallis doubted the outcome of the struggle from the start and worried how to survive this cataclysm of war and revolution. Intellectuals and defeatists are general labels, as they must be, for at the fringes (and sometimes in their midst) were people who did not wholly fit either description. Yet all those who argued for peace augmented the English government's desire for an accommodation with France.[94]

The list of those who actively sought peace with France is too long to be spelled out, but it is small compared with the many voices for peace with Germany. The appeal of appeasement was powerful precisely because a few intellectuals and defeatists stated its case so well.[95] Their motives were different, perhaps, but a Coleridge condemning war would have understood the opposition of Arnold Toynbee to a conflict with Germany. Cornwallis or Wilberforce could see eye to eye with Halifax or Lord Allen of Hurtwood in their despair of another holocaust. Other causes or interests were attracted to

---

[93] Feiling, *op. cit.*, p. 396, February, 1939.

[94] For Coleridge's views, see Samuel Taylor Coleridge, *Essays on his own times* (London, 1850), I, pp. 33, 153–154, 214; II, pp. 468–469, 583. Mrs. Henry Sandford *Thomas Poole and his friends* (London, 1888), I, pp. 221–222; II, p. 74. David V. Erdman, *Blake: Prophet against Empire* (Princeton, 1954), *passim*.

[95] Watt, "Influence from Without: German Influence on British Opinion, 1933–1938...," in *Personalities and Policies*, pp. 117–135.

appeasement, but certain intellectuals in each period believed appeasement to be right because war was so wrong. This moral sensitivity, which is courage too, seemed to justify them. The defeatists, discouraged from the start, had a more limited claim: to protect the established system. Here again the similarities are striking, but the combination of war and revolutionary circumstances created its distinctive terrors.

Passing from the appeal of appeasement to a consideration of its stages, it is possible to distinguish between an active and a passive phase each time. The phenomenon is recognizable in the 1930's and has been commented on. "Baldwin had favored appeasement; Chamberlain was determined to put it into practice," noted the authors of *The Appeasers*.[96] The Baldwin government, for a variety of reasons, avoiding committing itself too entirely to a policy of concessions. It played as much for time as for German friendship. Not Chamberlain, who rushed letters and emissaries to Rome and Berlin. It is not unwarranted to consider the Pitt/Addington administrations in a similar perspective. From 1795 till he resigned in 1801, Pitt intermittently sought peace, but it may be argued that he neither pushed too strenuously nor conceded sufficiently to obtain it. Addington initiated his government by announcing his intentions to make peace with France, and his foreign secretary actively pursued this object. Though Pitt had tried (and failed) for six years Addington carried the point in six months. The active appeasement of France brought the results which had eluded the cautious policies of the Pitt cabinet.

Even more interesting are the similar frustrations that develop following the settlements at Amiens and Munich. Both occasions produced second thoughts in London (almost immediately after the event in 1802, and within eight months of Munich) and diplomatic efforts to achieve a better balance through a coalition with Russia. The very reluctant overtures of the Chamberlain government during its discussions with the Soviet Union are too well known to need repeating here. Ideological fears and suspicions, and appeasement's latent hopes for an agreement on Poland, prevented these talks from coming to fruition. In 1802, Lord Hawkesbury, the foreign secretary, entertained similar plans. Initially he sought to construct an Anglo-Austro-Russian alliance, but Vienna's indolence soon made him concentrate his efforts on St. Petersburg. Russia, however, was not interested and nothing came of the project, though Hawkesbury continued trying to enlist the Russians against the French.[97]

[96] Gilbert and Gott, *The Appeasers*, p. 51. See also George A. Lanyi, "The Problem of Appeasement," *World Politics*, XV (January, 1963), p. 319.
[97] H. Beeley, "A Project of Alliance with Russia in 1802," *The English Historical Review*, XLIX (1934), pp. 497–502.

The failure to redress the balance of power in 1802 and 1939 with a Russian alliance did not affect the basic circumstances of appeasement. England had gone to the outer limits of concession, but her opponents were only at the beginning of their expansion. There followed a set of events sufficiently similar to speak of identical British reactions. Bonaparte ignored the provisions of the Treaty of Lunéville, and kept his troops in the Low Countries and northern Italy. In the fall of 1802 he interfered in Switzerland and rejected out of hand all British protests. But when he insisted that the English soldiers evacuate Malta, as they must under the provisions of Amiens, he ran into a wall of insular tenacity. The London government would make no more concessions. It insisted on retaining Malta (as compensation for Bonaparte's acquisitions) even if this meant war.

Hitler acted no better after Munich. He had barely absorbed the Sudetenland before reaching for Danzig and the Corridor. The British acquiesced in the unfair boundary settlements about the rump of Czechoslovakia; they accepted reluctantly the demise of the state which they had guaranteed six months before. But after the occupation of Prague they were no longer in the mood for concessions. Wisely or not, they guaranteed Poland and remained steadfast in their decision. Being stubborn about Malta was no more effective in halting aggression than standing by Poland's side. The English, however, were concerned with principles, and convinced themselves that their goodwill had been abused. Many writers have commented on this sudden reversal of British policy from flexible diplomacy to rigid stand, and traditionally it has been argued that British patience had been exhausted.

What happened, however, was not so simple. Publicly, the appeasement of Germany could no longer be defended after the occupation of Prague, but Chamberlain continued to work in private for better Anglo-German relations. He hoped to achieve this by settling German-Polish problems peacefully. Since neither Hitler nor Colonel Beck, the Polish foreign minister, would play this game Chamberlain's hidden appeasement was doomed. Similarly, the Addington cabinet tried to negotiate with Bonaparte about Malta. In its final proposal the English government limited itself to a temporary occupation of the island, acknowledged the independence of Malta, and requested the cession of the islet of Lampedusa (which belonged to the Neopolitan kingdom).[98] Despite two months of conversations Napoleon

---

[98] *Authentic Official Documents relative to the Negotiation with France ... as laid before both Houses of Parliament* (London, 1803), pp. 143-144, No. 68, Lord Hawkesbury to Lord Whitworth, May 7, 1803. The hidden appeasement of Chamberlain after March 15 is covered in detail by Gilbert and Gott, *The Appeasers*, pp. 233-298.

would not consider this offer. It was "Malte ou la guerre"; the English must evacuate the island. Diplomacy had failed.

Each time appeasement was abandoned with less speed than has been supposed. But abandoned it was, and the reasons are clear. The period of large concessions was over. Britain was still willing to negotiate but she would not concede without receiving something in return. It was also dawning on the British people that with their continued aggression Bonaparte and Hitler had destroyed the ideological justifications for their policies. Bonaparte had neither destroyed jacobinism (as the Addington cabinet thought) nor revived it (as the English feared). Instead, he had mobilized jacobin energies in the service of French imperialism. After the Czechs had lost their freedom Hitler could neither blame the treaty of Versailles nor explain his actions as the right of all Germans to self-determination. Nazism had shown its face, just as Bonaparte departed from the ideals of the jacobins. This realization made appeasement impossible and left the British obstinate.

Both tyrants may have sensed a change in attitude without comprehending it. Why was Britain so unyielding now? It may seem odd, but each voiced his frustrations in the same way. When in early 1803 relations between England and France deteriorated, Bonaparte sent for the British ambassador. Lord Whitworth called on the First Consul on February 18 at the Tuileries Palace, and was treated to a two-hour harangue. According to Lord Whitworth's dispatch he had little chance to contribute to the conversation, but Bonaparte's words were unmistakable. Unless Britain observed the treaty of Amiens (which meant she had to evacuate Malta), he was determined to attempt an invasion of her shores. He would personally assume command of such an expedition, Bonaparte declared, even when the chances were that he might go to the bottom of the sea. Though his odds were a hundred to one against him, he would proceed with this enterprise. If war came, army after army would be ready for an assault on the British isles. France had four hundred and eighty thousand men at her disposal. Clearly Bonaparte intended to use them, Whitworth concluded, for he had talked incessantly about his plans.[99]

At the brink of World War II a Swedish friend of Goering, Birger Dahlerus, was briefly used as intermediary between Berlin and London. In one of his meetings with Hitler, Dahlerus was asked by the Führer about the years he had lived in England. Having barely started with his reply, Hitler grew very excited and asserted that Germany was "irresistible." He was soon screaming

---

[99] *Authentic Official Documents*, pp. 70–74, No. 38, Lord Whitworth to Lord Hawkesbury, February 21, 1803.

If there should be war, then I shall build U-boats, build U-boats, U-boats, U-boats, U-boats ... I shall build aeroplanes, build aeroplanes, aeroplanes, aeroplanes, and I shall annihilate my enemies.[100]

A few days later, for good measure, Hitler shouted in Dahlerus' face

If England wants to fight for a year, I shall fight for a year; If England wants to fight two years, I shall fight two years ... If England wants to fight for three years, I shall fight for three years ... And, if necessary, I will fight for ten years.[101]

These words merely echoed what had been said before.

A last look at historical similarity may seem whimsical, focussing as it does on the odd aspects of the question. But the wide variety of points which can be raised justify that these be discussed. There is, for instance, the use of nearly identical words and phrases to describe the appeasement of France and Germany. Expressions like "peace at any price" and "peace with honor" are not just used in the twentieth century but in earlier times too. An editorial of William Cobbett addressed Addington in the following manner: "You and your partizans of 'peace on any terms' ..."[102] During the debate in the House of Commons on the preliminaries of peace, Fox was led to say "that the people were so goaded by the war, that they preferred peace almost upon any terms."[103] It hardly needs to be emphasized that "peace at any price" was a common expression in the newspapers of the 1930's, and has become firmly associated in the popular mind with appeasement. Again, when Chamberlain addressed the jubilant crowds outside No. 10 Downing Street, and spoke of "Peace with honour," he was not only quoting Disraeli but repeating Pitt's and Addington's words about the peace with France.[104]

If such phrases seem empty, either because they are meaningless or because these are the stock in trade of English political life, their nearly identical usage remains a matter of curiosity and surprise. Even more astonishing is the

---

[100] As quoted in Alan Bullock, *Hitler. A Study in Tyranny*, revised edition (New York, Bantam paperback, 1961), p. 482.

[101] *Ibid.*, p. 491.

[102] *Cobbett's Weekly Political Register*, March 20, 1802, p. 265.

[103] *The Parliamentary History of England*, Vol. 36 (London, 1820), p. 75. The Earl of Stanhope, in his biography of Pitt, asserts that Fox and his followers were regarded as so proFrench "that they gave some handle to the popular reproach of that time applied to them, as clamorous for 'peace upon any terms'," Earl Stanhope, *Life of the Right Honourable William Pitt* (London, 1862), III, p. 214.

[104] Feiling, *op. cit.*, p. 381; *Parliamentary History*, 36, pp. 12, 17. Pitt, in debate on the Address of Thanks to the King's Speech, had called the preliminaries "glorious and honourable." Lord Hawkesbury used the same expressions. *Ibid.*, 36, pp. 39, 41, 45. Addington, in a speech on the definitive treaty, stated "that he had not tarnished the honour of the country by the measures he had adopted..." *Ibid.*, 36, p. 812.

similar outburst of public hysteria which greeted the messengers of peace in 1801 and 1938. The London crowd went wild with joy when on October 10, General Lauriston, carrying the articles of ratification (of the peace preliminaries), arrived in London. The mob unhitched the horses of his carriage and pulled it through the streets.[105] Chamberlain's return to London on September 30, 1938 evoked a like outburst of joy, but it is not recorded that the populace insisted on pushing his automobile. Each time the genuine happiness with the peace overshadowed all else.

More interesting, perhaps, was a charge levelled by the journalist William Cobbett. In an open letter addressed to Lord Hawkesbury, and published in his *Weekly Political Register*, the cabinet was accused of preferring a peace treaty, which gave Great Britain no commercial advantages, to continuing the war "which would, probably, have lessened their present emoluments..." In other words, the government signed a disadvantageous agreement so that it might continue in office.[106] It is curious that such charges surfaced again in the 1940's. The controversy grew out of Baldwin's "utmost frankness" speech when he attempted to explain Britain's failure to rearm.

Supposing I had gone to the country and said that Germany was rearming, and that we must rearm, does anybody think that this pacific democracy would have rallied to that cry at that moment? [i.e., 1933] I cannot think of anything that would have made the loss of the election from my point of view more certain.[107]

Winston Churchill has cited this passage to accuse Baldwin of not having "done his duty in regard to national safety because he was afraid of losing the election...," although he absolves him of "any ignoble wish to remain in office." Since then historians have cleared Baldwin of this charge because the quote was misinterpreted by Churchill.[108] Chamberlain too had his reasons

---

[105] William Cobbett, *A collection of facts and observations relative to the peace with Bonaparte, etc.* (London, 1801), p. 66; *The Life and Letters of William Cobbett in England and America* (London, 1913), I, pp. 131–132.

[106] [William Cobbett], "To the Rt. Hon. Lord Hawkesbury," *Cobbett's Weekly Political Register*, April 17, 1802, p. 404. It is ironic that more than a century later an historian believed that the Addington cabinet resumed the war with France in 1803, because "the ministry was principally interested in its own preservation." See Harold C. Deutsch, *The Genesis of Napoleonic Imperialism* (Cambridge, Mass., 1938), p. 141.

[107] Stanley Baldwin, speaking in the House of Commons on November 12, 1936, and quoted in Winston S. Churchill, *The Gathering Storm* (Boston, 1948), p. 216. Churchill could not refrain in his memoirs from commenting that this statement carried frankness "into indecency." *Loc. cit.*

[108] Churchill, *Gathering Storm*, p. 216 For the refutation of the charge see R. Bassett, "Telling the truth to the people: The myth of the Baldwin 'Confession'," *The Cambridge Journal*, II (November 1948), pp. 84–95; J. H. Grainger, *Character and Style in English Politics* (Cambridge, 1969), pp. 174–177; Robert R. James, *Churchill: A Study in Failure, 1900–1939* (New York, 1970), pp. 293–297.

to justify his staying on. He wanted "a few more years," for otherwise "Liberals" would plunge the country "into a bloody and ruinous war."[109] Clearly, what was barely more than a press libel in Cobbett's day had by the 1930's grown to self-serving motives: success at the polls and in office had to precede the introduction of sound defense or foreign policies.

Because appeasement is forever associated with extravagant concessions, it is hardly surprising that each time bribery was tried as a last resort to keep the peace. In 1803 Lord Whitworth was moved by the thought of a new war to suggest paying the members of the Bonaparte family (and Talleyrand too) one or even two million pounds sterling. The cost would be minimal compared with the expenditures for one campaign. These efforts failed, however. Again, in late spring and summer 1939, Anglo-German discussions appear to have produced an offer to "loan" Germany one billion pounds to aid her economy and help her convert to peace-time production. Hitler was no more susceptible to money than Bonaparte, and bribery again showed its limitations.[110] Perhaps such offers signaled the end of appeasement; to throw away one's money is every fool's prerogative but cannot be called a policy.

But it is surely odd that even similar names and places claim our attention. We will mention only two: Eden and Vansittart. William Eden, Lord Auckland was a politician and diplomat who served in Spain and the Netherlands. In 1798 he joined Pitt's administration as joint postmaster-general. One of his daughters nearly made him Pitt's father in law. He severely criticized Pitt's resignation in 1801 and continued in the Addington government as postmaster-general. Anthony Eden, Lord Avon began his career in politics by specializing in foreign affairs. He served as minister for League of Nations Affairs before becoming Secretary of State for Foreign Affairs in 1936. Anthony Eden remained in office when Baldwin retired, but sharp differences with Chamberlain over foreign policy led to his resignation in February 1938. Nicholas Vansittart was a joint Secretary of the Treasury in the Addington government who was sent on a special diplomatic mission to Berlin and Copenhagen in connection with the League of Armed Neutrality. His mission was unsuccessful until Nelson attacked the Danish fleet before Copenhagen. Robert Vansittart was Permanent Under-Secretary in the Foreign Office during the Baldwin-Chamberlain years. His staunch opposition to the ap-

---

[109] Feiling, *op. cit.*, p. 396, February, 1939.

[110] British Museum, Manuscript Room, "Liverpool Papers," Add. mss 38238, vol. 49, Lord Whitworth to Lord Hawkesbury, March 24, 1803. Also, Carl L. Lokke, "Secret Negotiations to Maintain the Peace of Amiens," *American Historical Review*, XLIX (October 1943–July 1944), pp. 55–64; Gilbert and Gott, *The Appeasers*, p. 224.

peasement of Germany (but not Italy) led to his removal from this position by Chamberlain.

The city of Dunkirk offers the appropriate opportunity to end this chapter. Everyone knows the heroic withdrawal from its beaches by the British army in 1940, after having abandoned all its equipment. Less known is the similar exercise by the Duke of York in 1793. As commander of the British expeditionary force he had laid siege to the town in the opening phases of the war against France. When the soldiers of the revolution came to its relief the English were forced to retreat in great haste to Belgium. The British army lost all its heavy guns and most of its supplies during the withdrawal. Admittedly, this has little connection with appeasement. But then there are not many countries which first strenuously resist going to war and then open its campaigns by losing its equipment at the outset. Such people surely cherish peace.

CHAPTER IV

IDEOLOGICAL *ANGST*

The previous chapter has already mentioned ideology as a motive for appeasement. Ideology is a controversial subject; it is also a subtle and powerful wellspring of action. Under the circumstances a full discussion of the influence of ideology on British policy seems justified. This will be no easy matter: the connection between motive and policy is a tenuous one but the relationship between ideology and appeasement has frequently been denied altogether. As an element of British politics ideology has been mostly unpopular. It has been denounced as a foreign import whose "damnable principles" tended to corrupt "the lower ranks" and "the British constitution." Such attitudes of course ignored the many English pamphleteers who proposed radical changes and among whom Thomas Paine was the most strident.

A closer look at ideology during the 1790's and 1930's – the periods when appeasement hardened into a policy – will reaffirm the strong link between its role and revolution. Ideology per sé was neither new nor necessarily a cause for concern, but when combined with a dynamic political movement it became a fearsome crusade. Since these upheavals took place in a Europe that was unable or unwilling to resist, the ideological victories occurred with startling rapidity. The *ancien régime* could not muster a vigorous response to jacobinism; likewise, societies ravaged by World War I and the depression were in no state to marshal defenses against communism and nazism. The nexus of ideology and revolution may account for the rapid dissemination of its program, but it does not explain its attraction. In terms of appeal, ideology has gained its followers on its own merits.

To take our argument one step further, ideology has played a larger role in the history of the continent than in Great Britain. England has certainly had her share of great thinkers and philosophical systems, but that is not the same as ideology. The influence of her political philosophers was slight and their ideas were derivative of changes that had already taken place. There is no equivalent in British history of a jacobin, marxist or nazi movement gaining power first in one country and then sweeping half a continent off its feet. It is beyond the scope of this study to determine why ideology would capture so many European hearts and minds. In comparison with England and the long span of her political maturation in the eighteenth century, one is struck by the lack of the same political experience anywhere on the continent. What ideology offers are "inspired answers" to society's problems which politically more seasoned minds might question; it fosters the rapid change, the frog leap into modernity, but in the process of shedding worn-out habits politics as an art of the possible is cast aside.

The very nature of ideology (which will be discussed elsewhere) makes it unattractive to most Englishmen. "... in our Hearts we are all Politicians" writes one English woman to another and herein lies much of the answer.[1] The tendency to debate, to discuss public issues freely and to criticize the government grew steadily during the eighteenth century. English society was not a paradise of freedom but it contained a strong element of pragmatism. As such the principles of the counting house competed with the philosophic strictures of Edmund Burke, and his disciple William Windham complained bitterly about this mercantile outlook.[2] In a crisis the practical approach would prevail: Pitt rejected a royalist crusade against France just as firmly as Baldwin avoided any involvement in the Spanish civil war. "Englishmen should not fill their bellies with the east wind of German Socialism and Russian Communism and French Syndicalism."[3]

What Pitt said about a particular Burke letter "in which there is much to admire, and nothing to agree with" nicely epitomizes England's attitude toward ideology.[4] Burke might thunder against the French revolution and be listened to with respect, Windham could warn about the perils of parliamentary reform in the midst of the hurricane, yet neither could convince the country to think in ideological terms. No wonder Burke cursed war for the Scheldt as war for a chamberpot. The violation of a treaty (opening the estuary of the Scheldt river, closed by international agreement to all but the Dutch) by the French was the breaking of a contract. In the commercial circles of the City, the legal chambers of Gray's Inn, the lobbies of the House of Commons that was an offense about which one could wax indignant. But war over an "armed doctrine," a philosophic system was beyond the

---

[1] *The Francis Letters*, ed. by B. Francis (New York, no date), II, p. 484 Harriet Francis to Mary Johnson, September 25, 1801.

[2] *Life and Letters of Sir Gilbert Elliot, First Earl of Minto*, (London, 1874), II, p. 385, note 1 William Windham to Sir Gilbert Elliot, January 27, 1795.

[3] Baldwin as quoted in J. H. Grainger, *Character and Style in English Politics* (Cambridge, 1969), p. 167.

[4] *The Journals and Correspondence of William, Lord Auckland*, III, p. 320 Mr. Pitt to Lord Auckland, November 8, [1795].

Englishman's ken. Even if he understood its dangers he found it difficult to respond. [5]

If Pitt found it impossible to conduct ideological warfare, Baldwin and Chamberlain were no better at it. Both men had been appalled by the divisive prospects of the General Strike in 1926. Baldwin would strive to restore social harmony by stressing England's particular democratic traditions and shy away from any situation that might introduce ideological problems. In the 1930's that wasn't easy but he hoped "if there is any fighting in Europe to be done, I should like to see the Bolsheviks and the Nazis doing it."[6] Chamberlain had little of Baldwin's cultural pessimism; his way of dealing with ideology was to minimize it. That meant excluding Russia from his political horizon and looking at Germany in a conventional, business-like way. Berlin was "a rising market" and he hoped to deal by establishing a list of its needs which could be checked off pencil in hand. [7]

Has this ideological naiveté kept Great Britain free or left her more vulnerable? Despite social agitation and unrest during the 1790's and 1930's her government did not yield to any "system." But England's social structure seemed an easy target, her economic inequalities were obvious, and her empiricism was no match for the twin dangers of ideology and revolution. If French principles did not succeed in 1797, these were nevertheless in evidence at the fleet mutinies that year and Pitt, once more engaged in peace negotiations, must have wondered whether the republicans in Paris were a greater menace than the sailors of the King's navy who blockaded London. Similarly, Baldwin and Chamberlain could not avoid looking over their shoulder as they attempted to negotiate and rearm simultaneously. Would labor accept the costs and be willing to forego the social services that the state could not afford concurrently? How would the unions respond? The ideological issues may have been muted, but they could never be forgotten. Even the middle classes resisted paying higher taxes for rearmament.[8] In fact, the cabinet worried about pacifism and socialism at home as it kept a weary eye on communists and nazis abroad. Chamberlain may not have grasped England's ideological vulnerability but his policies were tinged with fear of it.

---

[5] William Wilberforce, after reading Thomas Paine's *Age of Reason*, could only exclaim "God defend us from such poison." *The Life of William Wilberforce*, by his sons Robert Isaac and Samuel Wilberforce (London, 1838), II, p. 61.

[6] Keith Middlemas and John Barnes, *Baldwin. A Biography* (New York, 1970), pp. 947, 955.

[7] Keith Feiling, *The Life of Neville Chamberlain* (London, 1946), p. 329; Martin Gilbert and Richard Gott, *The Appeasers* (Boston, 1963), p. 52.

[8] For concern about the unions, see Keith Middlemas, *Diplomacy of Illusion: The British Government and Germany, 1937–39* (London, 1972), p. 15; for middle class opposition to higher taxes for rearmament, see Feiling, *op. cit.*, pp. 292–293.

Ideology is a pregnant word. Its frequent use in the preceding paragraphs calls for an attempt to explain it.[9] If one accepts ideology's essential secularity, and thus by implication excludes religion, the ideological phenomenon can be described as modern, i.e., as first appearing in the eighteenth century. Above all else ideology is most explicit in its formulations and deals with a wide range of objects. Such doctrines are authoritative for its followers. Ideology tends to be highly systematized and unified around one or two supreme values, like social and economic equality, or ethnic and racial purity. The individual follower must be completely subservient to the ideological system; additionally, his life and conduct are expected to be permeated by it. Ideology is exclusive, emphasizing its distinctiveness from other beliefs or philosophies which may exist at the same time or place, and it will strongly resist any attempt to influence or modify its formulations. Its adherents must be in complete agreement with each other. A corporate organization enforces discipline among the committed, both for retaining loyalty and gaining new converts.

The dissemination of such principles are attended by emotional as well as rational overtones. Those who propagate ideologies always claim to speak for a higher existence, an ideal value which goes beyond the mere body of the faithful. This ideal, divergent from the here and now, strives for the realization of conditions which never existed at all, or were lost in the distant past. An ideology will be propelled by a strong sense of urgency about its application and hence involved with the exercise of power. Given this imperative it cannot help being political. This concentration on politics encompasses everything, but the final conditions are oppressive and undemocratic. Since ideology is the outgrowth of man's wish to impose a new intellectual order on the world, its alienation from the existing modes in society is a foregone conclusion. It hardly needs to be added that ideology and empiricism are totally incompatible.

So brief a sketch would mean little were it not for the French revolution to provide the testing ground for ideology. The changes in the French government were initially an internal affair without ideological overtones. Only after the conflict between the king and the national assembly, involving among other things the church and religion, had spilled across the borders to involve Austria and then Prussia, did the revolution assume a European significance. The outbreak of war in 1792 only highlights the expansion of the revolution in a political and military sense. In the realm of the mind the revolution had long since travelled across the continent and the Channel.

---

[9] This section owes a great deal to the excellent two-part article "Ideology" in *International Encyclopedia of the Social Sciences*, ed. David L. Sills (1968), VII, pp. 66–85.

The intellectual impact of events in France was immense. For Charles Fox the revolution was a joyful event, for Burke one of watchful waiting, and Goethe too had his forebodings while young Hegel celebrated the birth of liberty. If the work of the national assembly set an inspiring example for local patriots elsewhere to emulate, some of its changes, especially those involving the religious orders or the power of the king, began to disturb conservatives like Burke. England had experienced the growth of a reform movement independent of events in France; at one point even William Pitt had favored certain changes in the franchise for the House of Commons. The traditions of a free press had allowed a vigorous printing output on behalf of parliamentary reforms, while the events in Paris seemed to indicate what a free people could accomplish in an enlightened age. Then things began to go wrong on both sides of the Channel. In France the revolution undertook those changes which brought it into conflict with the crown, and eventually with foreign states. In England the tone of certain publications, especially of Thomas Paine, and the fact that "the lower ranks" were reading six-penny prints of *The Rights of Man* frightened the establishment.[10]

As the revolution in France moved from relatively moderate positions to radical solutions, politics began to assume an ideological tone. No doubt the worsening domestic situation – rising food prices, shortages, civil unrest – and the growing threat of a counterrevolution contributed to the demands for greater equality and limitations on the executive power. But the outbreak of war in April, 1792, really sealed the fate of the monarchy since the conflict with Austria was attributed to the intrigues of Marie Antoinette.

To a certain extent the egalitarian ideology of the revolution had been present from the beginning. At first only a tiny minority had espoused such views. Then the declaration of war set off a chain of events – invasion of France, massacres in Paris, abolition of the monarchy – which transformed a limited, partisan struggle into something else. The ideological warfare that was conducted by the republic was part fact, part fiction. It depended as much on foreign sympathizers as its own rhetoric. When the war effort faltered ideological requirements were most strenuous at home, when the French armies succeeded ideology would be introduced abroad. By the fall of 1792 the struggle had changed from the traditional warfare of the eighteenth

---

[10] See the fascinating exchange between the keelman of Shields and General Lambton in *The Life of William Wilberforce*, II, pp. 2, 3–4. Sales estimates for *The Rights of Man* fluctuate between 200,000 and 1,500,000, but even the lower figure compares favorably with Burke's *Reflections on the Revolution in France* which sold no more than 30,000 copies. R. R. Palmer, *The Age of the Democratic Revolution*, vol. II The Struggle (Princeton, 1964 paperback ed.), p. 476.

century, but the ideological offensive was neither as well organized nor as monolithic as the enemies of the republic assumed.[11]

Nevertheless, the promulgation of two propaganda decrees in November and December, on the face of it, threatened the existing social order. The first "promised aid and friendship to all peoples who wished to attain liberty"; the second declared that "when French forces entered enemy lands, commanders would proclaim the abolition of tithes and feudal dues, abolish aristocratic privilege, convoke primary assemblies . . . and confiscate the property of the ruling prince, the Church, and the aristocrats."[12] The republic may have intended to deal only with the Belgian situation and the doubtful loyalty of General Dumouriez, but the language of the decrees did not indicate that. Moreover, the French confused national security with protection for ideological sympathizers in countries bordering on the republic, and ended up by annexing Savoy and Belgium. Private assurances to England and Switzerland that the propaganda decrees did not have universal application did little to set London at rest when public action by the French armies violated treaties and established interests.

European observers of the French republic were reluctant to draw a distinction between aid for Italian or Rhineland democrats and national expansion. But by now domestic events in France as much as foreign opposition led the Convention to declare war on England, Spain and Holland simultaneously. Sardinia, Prussia and Austria were already at war with the republic. This defiance of Europe by the "Iron Republic" (Burke) opened the gates for the period of the Terror and forever associated the name Jacobin with the egalitarian ideology. In fact, ideology had preceded and would survive the regime of Robespierre, but "armed doctrine" and the French republic had become synonymous. The republicans may not have sought the subversion of Europe; the success of the French armies convinced every conservative nevertheless that nothing was sacred or safe and that a restoration of the *ancien régime* could only be accomplished with the defeat of the revolution.

Across the Channel the British watched these earth-shaking events with fascination and horror. At the official level the cabinet observed a strict neutrality: England had not signed the Declaration of Pillnitz, she refused when requested to join a coalition against France, and the English government was the first to recognize the constitution of 1791 which made France a

---

[11] Palmer, *op. cit.*, II, pp. 10–16, 50–65.
[12] Steven T. Ross, *European Diplomatic History 1789–1815: France Against Europe* (Garden City: Anchor paperback, 1969), pp. 61, 63.

constitutional monarchy. In 1792 Pitt reduced the military budget, declaring that he expected fifteen years of peace, and when war broke out two months later the government again rejected requests by the Bourbon princes for intervention against the revolution. [13] Burke had a chance to see Pitt, but he found him more interested in Poland, or even China, "than in nipping a world revolution in the bud," and Lord Auckland complained that the prime minister and his foreign secretary were behaving like "spectators in a theatre." [14]

This equanimity did not really tell the depth of British concern. Revolution in Paris which demoralized this archrival was one thing, but a foreign revolution that might serve as inspiration for England's own "jacobins" was a very disturbing matter. Even Pitt worried about who might be learning the wrong things because he warned his brother, the First Lord of the Admiralty, that Paine's works were being read in the dockyards. The Commissioners should be given instructions to put a stop to this. [15] Subversive publications were not the only cause for concern, but enough for the government to take the first step against such agitation. In May, 1792, it issued a proclamation banning seditious writings. The measure was especially directed against Paine. He fled to France and became a French citizen. His departure did not quiet the demands for reform but posed anxious questions about the contacts between English reformers and French republicans. How widespread was the sentiment scribbled on a garden wall: "No coach-tax; damn Pitt! damn the Duke of Richmond! no King!" [16]

A letter of William Elliot of Wells, close friend of Burke and later a member of the House of Commons, reveals the tension of those November days. "The object of the modern fanatic," he says, "is of entirely a different nature. It is much more capacious and comprehensive in its tendency. Their scheme amounts to the total and complete subversion of all existing institutions and establishments." Could England's agitators accomplish this unaided?

[13] *The Cambridge Modern History*, vol. 8 The French Revolution (New York, 1907), p. 296. The question whether Pitt used secret service money to influence events in France surreptitiously is denied in a recent article by Howard V. Evans, "The Nootka Sound Controversy in Anglo-French Diplomacy – 1790," *The Journal of Modern History*, 46 (December, 1974), pp. 609–640.

[14] Arthur Bryant, *The Years of Endurance, 1793–1802* (London, 1961, Fontana paperback), p. 91. Lord Auckland as quoted in Carl B. Cone, *Burke and the Nature of Politics*, vol. 2 The Age of the French Revolution (Lexington, 1964), p. 378.

[15] E. Keble Chatterton, *England's Greatest Statesman: A Life of William Pitt, 1759–1806* (Indianapolis, 1930), pp. 247–248.

[16] *Life and Letters of Sir Gilbert Elliot*, II, p. 71 Lady Malmesbury to Lady Elliot, [October–November], 1792.

The French are part of the seditions in every country; this is their mode of conquest ... When once political seduction is systematically practised, armies and navies will be but brittle weapons ... England, I much dread, must expect her share of the calamity. Recent examples prove that no government can resist the insurrection of its own subjects without at the same time encountering France.[17]

His conclusions were that "subordinate reforms are worse than useless; they betray weakness and timidity on the part of the Government without conciliating the mind of a single insurgent. To concede, therefore, at this moment is to surrender."

Though William Elliot may have been under Burke's spell, he was known as a sober young man of considerable intelligence. If English conditions and French policies could incite such feelings in a person like him, it is no wonder that the majority of the articulate establishment supported the government's policy of calling a halt to French expansion in the low countries. War might not be wanted but it could stop the ominous drift of the popular mind. It would be difficult to document such speculations, even if a moderate like Christopher Wyvill would accuse Pitt of giving the people war instead of the parliamentary reform that they had sought.[18]

But whether war was used to frustrate ideology or not, England could not check its influence. Throughout the nineteenth century the challenges of revolution and "the social question" continued to disturb existing regimes as the egalitarian ideology made new converts in each generation. The formation of a new ideology concerned with economic justice complemented the goals of the French revolution. At the same time, romanticism and social darwinism furnished the bases for an ideology of racial purity which was particularist rather than universal in its appeal. The twentieth century would become the battleground for both ideologies.

The outbreak of revolution in Russia was greeted instantly as a liberating event. Now the eastern ally of the Entente powers would stand for the same democratic ideals in the struggle against Prussian militarism. Before the year was out these hopes had vanished as the communist party came to power and Russia left the war. At least one Englishman had been dubious from the start. Neville Chamberlain recorded in his diary on April 22, 1917: "This Russian revolution, which by a grim sort of irony is received everywhere with shouts of approval by our people as though it were going to win the war for us, is

[17] *Ibid.*, II, pp. 73–74 William Elliot of Wells to Sir Gilbert Elliot, November, 19, 1792, also pp. 36–37.

[18] Christopher Wyvill, *Political Papers* (York, 1794–1802), IV (1802), p. 74 "The Case of the Reverend C. Wyvill," April 16, 1796.

fermenting all the unsteady brains of the world."[19] This attitude may not have been general in 1917, but a year later English troops were at Murmansk and Archangel, in a virtual state of war with the Bolshevik government. Although this intervention would end soon, its principal author, Winston Churchill, excoriated communist ideology as "the nameless beast" and "a sub-human structure."[20]

It would serve no purpose to demonstrate at length the basic hostility of each Conservative government to communism. The first Labor cabinet seem-ed more sympathetic to the Soviet régime, but MacDonald's tenure of power was too brief to change attitudes or policies. The depressed post-war economy boosted the desire for trade with Russia, even communist Russia, but the promise of this vast market never materialized. Renewed contacts with Russia led to the opening of a Russian trade mission in London with all the opportunities for underhanded activities. The dissatisfaction of labor, persistent unemployment, the growing number of strikes culminating in the 1926 General Strike, and the affair of the spurious Zinoviev letter were all symptoms that disturbed the public. The Conservative party had never had any doubts about the enmity of communism. In 1924 it convinced a majority of the electorate that the first Labor government could not be trusted to deal effectively with possible subversion directed from abroad. This conservative victory set the official tone of Britain's response to communism for the next fifteen years.

The five years of Conservative government parallel the post-war recovery in European history. The Locarno pact notwithstanding, it was an unsettling time for many Englishmen. For one thing, it was now clear that Britain's economic decline could not be reversed without major changes. Should she abandon free trade? Could she maintain a profitable link with her empire whose ties were slipping? At home a nagging underemployment stimulated labor unrest; the fear of losing one's job in a shrinking labor market was widespread. The spectre of social chaos evoked by the General Strike raised equivalent fears among the ranks of the middle and upper class. Was this how it had started in 1917? The attitude of social reconciliation promoted by Stanley Baldwin after the strike helped to bridge the chasms that had opened in British society. It also muffled any ideological sounds that threatened to distract Englishmen.

The Depression inaugurated a decade of turmoil. For Great Britain it

[19] Feiling, *op. cit.*, pp. 79–80.
[20] Robert Rhodes James, *Churchill: A Study in Failure, 1900–1939* (New York, 1970), pp. 134, 171. Winston S. Churchill, *The Aftermath* (New York, 1929), p. 61. Winston S. Churchill, *The Unknown War* (New York, 1932), p. 377.

meant a whole series of crises: staggering numbers of unemployed, budget deficits and cuts in the dole, the abandonment of the gold standard and free trade, the transformation of the empire to a commonwealth of nations, and lastly the Nazi revolution in Germany. A few months before the Wall Street crash Labor had once more been elected to office, but in two-years' time it had ruined its mandate. Its successor, the National Government, struggled vigorously to master the economic problems and to adjust its imperial relations. The 1931 election gave the Conservative party a clear majority – one that would hold till 1945 – and by 1937 Great Britain had experienced a moderate recovery from the Depression. Unemployment had been cut in half, exports were up, the pound sterling was stable, and there was a definite boom in home building.[21] The empire had been recast into a commonwealth of semi-independent states. These successes were the result of a very careful mixture of stimulating business and cutting expenditures: there was neither excessive pump priming nor a too rigid deflationary policy.

A high price was paid for these accomplishments. The limited recovery with its permanent unemployed of more than 1,300,000 left the public mood depressed and unappreciative.[22] The ministers in turn were worn out by their exertions to save the country and the pound. Both prime minister (Baldwin) and foreign secretary (Hoare) are known to have suffered from exhaustion and nervous collapse. They were ill-prepared to face one more debacle: the renaissance of a virulent Germany. The Nazi revolution that overtook Germany was not only ideological but extremely dynamic. The cautious Victorians governing England shrank from this incubus, wishing to deflect it from themselves.

How much of a threat was Nazi ideology? Since Nazism does not rank very high in intellectual contents it may seem a preposterous question. Could its authoritarian tone hold any attraction for democratic Englishmen? Still, this was the Depression, there were legions of unemployed and property owners were concerned about the security of their position. Would a growing movement on the left, fanned by economic distress, lead to a party of political extremism on the right? Even if it did not happen, for neither communism nor fascism ever gained a mass following, the potential for such extremes worried Baldwin if it could divide the country.[23] And if prime ministers harbored such

[21] W. H. Richardson, *Economic Recovery in Britain, 1932–1939* (London, 1967), pp. 21–22.

[22] John A. Garrary, "The New Deal, National Socialism and the Great Depression," *American Historical Review*, 78 (October, 1973), pp. 936–938.

[23] F. S. Northedge, *The Troubled Giant: Britain among the Great Powers, 1916–1939* (New York, 1966), pp. 385–386; Middlemas and Barnes, *Baldwin*, p. 967; Grainger, *op. cit.*, pp. 167–168.

ideological anxieties, would lesser lights in government or social circles be free from these fears?[24]

There was one further aspect in these ideological considerations. If the British government had frankly acknowledged from the beginning that communism was its enemy, the same could not be said for its response to nazism. This assertion does not imply that the National Government was pro-nazi; rather, at first its assessment of the new system in Germany was not to regard it as a calamity. Germany was once again rabidly nationalist, but unless it engaged in foreign adventures, what it did at home was its own business. This neutrality about nazism's ideological implications (as compared with communism) left many Englishmen confused and a tiny minority convinced that it had found the answer to Britain's problems. It also offered German propaganda opportunities in England which would not have been available if it had been realized earlier that Nazi ideology was "for export."[25]

No doubt the ideological challenge facing Britain in the twentieth century was more severe than in the 1790's. Then egalitarian ideology had defied a strongly hierarchical society and left a legacy despite its defeat in the short run. A nearly recovered (from the war with the American colonies) Britain had entered the war with the French republic and emerged vastly stronger twenty years later. Now a more democratic Britain, exhausted after World War I, faced a twin challenge of communist ideology and fascist arrogance. Could British democracy survive in the face of these dangers? Could she, deep in the Depression, afford to survive without fundamental changes in her way of life? The English cabinet had learned to live with the communist challenge which posed no immediate threat. Nazi dynamism was, however, another matter. Perhaps by ignoring its ideology one could arrive at a practical understanding. It seemed a reasonable assumption for one who could write, after reading *The House that Hitler Built*, "if I accepted the author's conclusions, I should despair, but I don't and won't,"[26] Here was the modern formula for dealing with ideology: to keep the first at arm's length while shutting one's mind (if not one's eyes) to the second!

So far our account has presented the ideological challenge. It is now England's response that must be examined in its turn. The trumpet blast from Paris proclaiming the rights of man, equality and liberty was answered by a

---

[24] For one illustration, see the interesting article by Donald Lammers, "Fascism, Communism and the Foreign Office, 1937–1939," *Journal of Contemporary History*, VI (1971), pp. 66–86.

[25] D. C. Watt, *Personalities and Policies. Studies in the Formulation of British Foreign Policy in the Twentieth Century* (South Bend, 1965), pp. 117–135.

[26] Feiling, *op. cit.*, p. 328.

lonely voice from across the Channel. Edmund Burke's was no *sotto voce* but for a long time his was a solo response. There were others, of course, but who remembers their subsidized pamphlets, books or newspaper diatribes? What makes Burke memorable is his genuine intellectual contribution to the great debate about man and society. When French ideologists called on natural law Burke evoked history, where they cited rights he pointed to customs and what they wished to reform he sought to preserve in the name of tradition. Because Burke appealed to the familiar, the known as against the experimental, his arguments sounded comforting to people frightened by the untried future and longing for the past. Although his theoretical system went against the trend of thought held modern in its day, Burke's conservatism became a true intellectual opponent of the egalitarian ideology. He remains the starting point for all conservative thinkers to this day.

His achievement is all the more remarkable because he wrote without official encouragement. He held no government sinecure or cabinet rank, and though a member of the House of Commons he was never close to Pitt and his circle. Many people, even if they agreed with his opposition to the French revolution, considered his tone intemperate and his language coarse. There was an air of potatoes and whiskey about Burke's oratory, said one contemporary.[27] The Whig party did not particularly appreciate him at this time (1790–'91) and the fact that he possessed a creative mind counted for little in a society more impressed with origins than originality. Despite his stand against the revolution, Burke did not participate in the struggle against French "ideas" in Britain. Hannah More's two-penny pamphlets, "Church and King" mobs and "Loyal Associations" were simpler perhaps but more effective than the arguments of this philosopher.

And yet Burke's counterrevolutionary arguments had a purpose: to launch all-out war against the French republic and to restore the Bourbon monarchy. He was virtually alone in urging Pitt to resist this egalitarian offensive with an ideological war of his own. Only one minister, William Windham, secretary at war, would espouse this cause; he was Burke's voice in the cabinet but he did not exercise much influence. In fact, what Burke preached Pitt would not follow. An ideological war to crush the revolution, to restore the Bourbons, was entirely beyond his capacities or inclinations.

Pitt and his foreign secretary, William Grenville, had strenuously resisted going to war. They had looked on quietly as France crumbled; the weakening of this archrival and the decline of the Bourbon dynasty did not disturb them. The cause of royal absolutism found no support in London; neither did the

---

[27] Bryant, *The Years of Endurance*, p. 74 footnote. The comment was made by John Wilkes.

war of Austria and Prussia against the new constitutional monarchy in France. Come what may, the English government tried to remain on good terms with the French. Moreover, domestic agitation did not yet worry the cabinet where it would blame foreign subversion for it. This careful policy was severely shaken by events in Paris during August and September, 1792. The violence in Paris, the abolition of the monarchy, and the first military triumphs of the republic presented the English ministers with a fundamental question: could the revolution be restricted to France? The capture of Brussels by General Dumouriez, and the proclamation of the Convention offering French assistance to all people (both events in November), warned that it might not.

War broke out in February, 1793, over the narrow issue of the opening of the Scheldt estuary to international trade. This step violated long-standing treaties which meant nothing to the French republicans. Pitt could argue that the war was just: Britain had gone to war in defense of her Dutch ally and the maintenance of international agreements. The absence of ideological rhetoric was understandable; Pitt himself was confused about the nature of the war. He thought it would be short and add more sugar islands to Britain's empire.[28] Much later, when the conflict had gone badly for England, he would explain that the object of the war was "security" and a more stable government in France. By then Great Britain was fighting for her very life and the war which Pitt had imagined – a short war in which her allies defeated France in Europe while she conquered French colonies – had long since proved a mirage.

What had happened? With revolutionary ardor France had defeated all armies sent against her. By 1795 Prussia had withdrawn from the First Coalition, Austria stood on the defensive and all English soldiers had been evacuated from the continent. These reverses alone would shake a government that had conducted a set piece war against an "armed doctrine." In fact, the war had been unpopular from the beginning and was denounced in Parliament and outside it. Between 1793 and 1795 the crescendo of protests mounted ever higher until in the latter year the King was shot at on his way to open Parliament. Outside the crowd shouted for peace, bread and Pitt's resignation, inside the small band of Foxites tirelessly introduced motions calling for negotiations with France. Windham summed it up a few years later

---

[28] *The Life of William Wilberforce*, II, pp. 10–11. A. W. Ward and G. P. Gooch, *The Cambridge History of British Foreign Policy, 1783–1919*, vol. I, 1783–1815 (Cambridge, 1939), pp. 219, 256.

when he told the House of Commons

Never was there a war carried on with such an incessant cry for peace from the very beginning of it. In any other war, would it have been tolerated that the justice of our cause should be incessantly arraigned, and that of the enemy defended, in newspapers and other publications; that everyone who endeavoured to rouse the public spirit would be villified and abused?

Yet what do I infer? Why, that such writings never could have obtained circulation, had there not been an indecision in the public mind on the subject of the war. It is with reluctance that I acknowledge this state of the public mind to have prevailed.[29]

If there was indecision in the public mind, it merely reflected what was in William Pitt's. He had stumbled into a war which was going from bad to worse. Abroad the French republic was largely victorious, at home criticism of the war was intense. To still the critics the government initiated a number of treason trials in 1794, but all the defendants were acquitted. Despite this setback, more repression soon followed but opposition to the war would continue nevertheless. By 1795 the nature of the war had changed; for Britain it was now a struggle for survival against an ideologically charged republic.

Pitt never came to grips with the demands of this contest. In an ordinary eighteenth century war he might have been successful, although Macaulay concluded that "his military administration was that of a driveller."[30] Neither Pitt nor Dundas were in the least suited to conduct an ideological war. As Secretary for War and the Colonies, and Pitt's political manager for Scotland, Dundas was the most powerful man in the cabinet besides the prime minister. But Dundas was primarily interested in empire and his efforts were wholly directed to conquering the enemy's colonies. Pitt meanwhile tried to steer a middle course ("tiding it over" Windham called it) between the demand for a crusade against France and the call for a reconciliation with her. In truth, he appeared at a loss what to do. He harbored no wish to restore the Bourbons but he also shrank from making peace at disadvantageous terms. This indecision brought England to the brink of disaster.

More than sixty years ago Pitt's biographer J. Holland Rose sought an answer to the question: "Why did not Pitt call the nation to arms?" In other words, why didn't he mobilize for total war to challenge this ideological foe? Professor Rose's words should speak for themselves.

---

[29] *The Parliamentary History of England from the Earliest Period to the Year 1803* (London, 1820), vol. 36, p. 750, May 13, 1802.

[30] Lord Macaulay, *Critical, Historical and Miscellaneous Essays* (Boston, 1860), VI, p. 275.

The reasons for his caution are doubtless to be found in the ingrained conservatism of the English character, and in the political ferment which marked the years 1794–'5. The mere proposal to merge Line, Militia, and Volunteers in one national array would have seemed mere madness. For the populace had recently been protesting against the facilities given to the loyal to arm and drill themselves. It was rumored that, by way of retort, the men of Sheffield, Southwark, and Norwich secretly mustered for practice with pikes. In such circumstances, conscription might well spell Revolution. Here was the weak place in Pitt's armour. By parting company with the reformers, he had embittered no small section of his countrymen.[31]

Here is the best glimpse of ideological *Angst* as it affected policy.

Since Pitt had immured himself from total war, he faced a piecemeal struggle without an end. Unaware of these complications he wavered between giving battle and negotiations with a republican régime which he had previously condemned. One illustration will serve to show Pitt's lack of purpose: the first attempt to start peace talks in 1795. In March Prussia had officially withdrawn from the First Coalition by signing the treaty of Basel; one month later the English expeditionary force was evacuated from northern Germany. Tuscany, Holland and Spain had been conquered or joined the other side. Yet on May 27, 1795, in opposing a Wilberforce peace motion, Pitt breathed defiance and declared "I will not acknowledge such [i.e., regicide] a Republic."[32] These brave words Pitt was to swallow five months later when the King's speech opening Parliament (October 29, 1795) proposed peace negotiations.

Perhaps Pitt's change of heart was induced by the new constitution and the end of the national convention in France. If such was the case he had ignored an important event. On October 1, 1795, the out-going convention by acclamation had voted for the decree on the natural frontiers of the republic, and this decision by the deputies became a part of the new constitution. Henceforth the Rhine and the Rhineland, Holland, Belgium and Luxembourg were an integral part of the French state.[33] Four weeks later Pitt extended the offer to negotiate. What followed in the next two years is well known: two separate missions of Lord Malmesbury to Paris and Lisle failed to obtain peace. After the first attempt, when Malmesbury was sent home, Burke, strongly opposed to negotiations, jeered: "This mongrel had been whipped back to the kennel yelping and with his tail between his legs."[34]

If Pitt had felt the need to make peace before, the second effort in 1797 took

---

[31] J. Holland Rose, *William Pitt and the Great War* (London, 1911), pp. 278–279.

[32] As quoted in Ward and Gooch, *op. cit.*, I, p. 261.

[33] Albert Sorel, *L'Europe et la Révolution française*, 11th ed. (Paris, 1918), IV, p. 431.

[34] J. Holland Rose, "Burke, Windham and Pitt," *English Historical Review*, XXVIII (1913), p. 105.

place under the most horrendous circumstances. The near failure of the Bank of England, several mutinies in the fleet, unrest among some regiments at Woolwich, continued popular unrest, poor harvests and high food prices – these were the conditions which forced Pitt once again to initiate conversations. Despite huge English concessions the talks failed. Pitt tried bribing the Directorate, briefly considered resigning and finally decided to continue the war. He had no alternative to outright surrender but to follow the same policies, only more so. A very large tax increase would pay for the war while stricter enforcement of the Two Acts (Traitorous Correspondence Bill, suspension of Habeas Corpus) was to prevent civil unrest. But it was obvious that the prime minister who could not make peace was equally unable to finish the war.

Bonaparte's coup d'état of November 9, 1799, introduced a new element in the stalemate. A general free of ideological complications might extinguish "the principles of exaggerated liberty" and "all systems of democratic equality." Would he prove to be a new General Monk and restore the Bourbons? Canning was convinced Bonaparte meant the end of the republic. "The idol of Jacobinism is no more," he crowed.[35] Windham felt less certain about Bonaparte's anti-jacobinism but both men, quite independently, were sure that peace negotiations with this new government, "starting from underneath the ground," were out of the question.[36] When an offer to negotiate was made, it was peremptorily rejected by a much criticized letter of Lord Grenville. His advice for Bonaparte to restore the Bourbons led to the obvious reply that France, in changing her government, was only following the English example.

Despite this unpromising start extended conversations with Bonaparte were held in 1800. The Austrian empire had signed a ceasefire with him and Pitt was eager to join the peace talks. The First Consul, however, demanded a naval armistice as the price for discussing terms. A naval truce would save the French army trapped in Egypt. This condition was unacceptable to the English government and the effort to open negotiations failed. These preliminary discussions served a useful purpose nevertheless. After seven years of war Pitt's cabinet had fractured to no less than five different opinions about

[35] These quotes are from Canning's letter of November 19, 1799, to his friend Lord Boringdon, in Augustus G. Stapleton, *George Canning and his times* (London, 1859), pp. 43–44. For another Canning letter of the same date, see Lord Granville Leveson Gower, *Private Correspondence, 1781–1821* (London, 1917), I, p. 273.

[36] For Canning, *loc. cit.; Select Speeches of the Rt. Honourable William Windham*, ed. by Robert Walsh (Philadelphia, 1837), p. 67. *The Windham Papers*, with an introduction by the Rt. Hon. the Earl of Rosebery (Boston, 1913), II, pp. 143–144 W. Windham to W. Pitt, November 18, 1799.

the issue of peace. A long memorandum of Dundas ranges from those who sought to restore the Bourbons and opposed any transaction which did not work for this object to ministers who were convinced that military action could no longer influence events in France, and that consequently negotiations ought to be taken up with the Consulate. Between these two extremes were partisans of peace talks of varying intensity.[37]

If part of the cabinet (the exact number is not known) had overcome its scruples about negotiating with republican France, the role of the First Consul was crucial. Canning was right that for the present Bonaparte spelled an end to ideological assaults. But Pitt's government was too divided to benefit from this turn of events; its resignation in early 1801 brought the necessary change for initiating discussions with France.[38] Pitt's cabinet may have foundered on its failure to obtain peace, or the emancipation of the Irish Catholics; probably both issues had divided the government so badly that its worn-out leader was only too glad to surrender the seals of office. His successor announced his commitment to peace and worried about a "jacobin" revival.[39] Since the new administration was weak and lacked experience it could not deal with daily problems in the offhanded manner that Pitt had been used to.

Henry Addington became prime minister when England longed for peace, rioted against high food prices and faced acute shortages. The victories before Copenhagen and Alexandria did little to change conditions at home. Nearly every day Addington received letters with bad news about the domestic scene. "I hold the Law of the Country totally overthrown ... and the mischief increases" wrote a general from the west of England. A clergyman of Yorkshire complained about "Dissenters ... with Jacobinical tenets" who "seduced the lower classes with their petition for peace." An M.P. for Devonshire reported grave unrest among the dockyard men, so organized "that the commissioners had thought it necessary to spike the cannon within the yard." But the most frequent and alarmist of these correspondents was Sir John Macpherson, Whig M.P., former governor general of India, and a rather strange busybody. As early as March, 1801, he warned the new prime minister "War, continued beyond a certain point, is but the vehicle of interior

---

[37] *English Historical Documents*, vol. XI, 1783–1832, ed. by A. Aspinall and E. Anthony Smith (London, 1959), pp. 110–111, "Henry Dundas's Memorandum on the State of the Cabinet," September 22, 1800.

[38] Pitt's resignation remains a controversial subject. For a recent discussion and some new documentation, see Richard Willis, "William Pitt's Resignation in 1801: Re-examination and Document," *Bulletin of the Institute of Historical Research*, 44 (November, 1971), pp. 239–257.

[39] George Pellew, *The Life and Correspondence of the Right Honble Henry Addington, First Viscount Sidmouth* (London, 1847), I, pp. 357–358, 361.

revolution." And again later, "the failure or delay [of peace] would plant the war in our bosom and with it the Revolutionary Revolts." For Macpherson Bonaparte was the guardian against jacobins and of peace.[40]

The impact on Addington of such news can only be surmised, but since related events moved him to act it may be assumed that he took the various alarms seriously. Thus he knew from Pitt himself that the war and the shortage of food were connected and that the government had been unable to solve this problem.[41] Scarcity was the mother of discontent and Addington had full knowledge how much discontent would arise if the war continued. He had immediately informed the country of his wish for peace and he acted promptly to begin discussions with the French commissioner for prisoner exchanges in London. Additional facts corroborate our thesis. The Portuguese government, England's oldest ally, had requested military assistance against Spain which had attacked Portugal at the behest of France. The Addington cabinet refused, citing its own security as the reason.[42] The pursuit of peace dictated this decision, for to act positively would offend France. Similarly, when Bonaparte made several preparations for the invasion of England, all intended to pressure her to come to terms, Addington took it seriously and complained that the newspapers were "too tame" about the danger of a landing.[43] Could he then ignore the warnings that revolution was possible if peace was not forthcoming? The road to Amiens may have been paved with good intentions but ideological anxiety grew all along the way.

Ideology was the new factor in the struggle between Britain and France; the nature of the war changed from one of limited objective to total defeat of the enemy. In the twentieth century, however, ideology has become an accepted fact of life: the word is used almost casually in referring to an individual's opinions or an organization's program. This habitual use had not promoted a thorough knowledge of the major ideological systems, however. In the

---

[40] The letters to Addington are in the "Addington MSS," Box 1801, Devon Record Office, Exeter, and Pellew, *op. cit.*, I, pp. 246–247, 362, 363, 448–452. There are more details about unrest in the dockyards in *Letters of Admiral of the Fleet, the Earl of St. Vincent*, ed. by David B. Smith (London, 1927), II, pp. 167–196, and Appendix, pp. 438ff. Sir John Macpherson reminds one of Baldwin's confidant Thomas Jones. Henry Richard, Lord Holland, *Memoirs of the Whig Party during my time* (London, 1852), I, p. 185.

[41] "...I own I see no adequate remedy" confessed Pitt in a letter of October 8, 1800, to Addington, in Pellew, *op. cit.*, I, p. 263.

[42] "Addington MSS," Box 1801, Devon Record Office, Exeter, Lord Hawkesbury to Marquis de Lima, July 15, 1801. *The Later Correspondence of George III*, ed. by A. Aspinall, vol. III, January 1798–December 1801 (Cambridge, 1967), p. 511 "Cabinet Minute."

[43] "Addington MSS," Box 1801, Devon Record Office, Henry Addington to Hiley Addington, August 29, 1801. *Letters of Admiral ... the Earl of St. Vincent*, I, pp. 121–122.

political world the advocacy or condemnation of communism, fascism or even racism are weapons with which to bludgeon one's opponents or arouse one's followers. Ideology has thus become the greatest challenge for the politician in this mass age – especially for the politician who claims to be free of ideological commitments. He will most likely be the spokesman of an old-fashioned society.

The establishment of communism, even in one country, by the end of World War I, detracted from the Allied war effort and cast a shadow over the promise of a better post-war world. In 1815 England had felt confident that the defeat of Napoleon removed the dangers of jacobinism. The defeat of Germany in 1918 gave her no similar assurances. To see the largest territorial state captured by an ideology so alien to the British system that it automatically became an enemy, was depressing indeed. The outcome of the civil war was further proof of communist tenacity. To be sure Russia was weak, and this condition lulled the politicians of the 1920's and '30's into the belief that as a military factor she could be discounted. But her potential for ideological mischief was great. Tory politicians made ample use of this to frighten the electorate, berate their Labor opponents and upset themselves.

The extension of the franchise in 1918 brought women into the electorate, but this political reform, or the long parliamentary tradition, could not hide the essentially undemocratic nature of English society and its economy. The rigid social hierarchy of Britain, the concentration of vast wealth in a few hands were easy targets for an ideological system advocating economic and social equality. The growing electoral importance of the Labor party was both new and disturbing to the conservative establishment. Although its program proposed only moderate reforms, opposition leaders like Winston Churchill consistently called the Laborites socialists. Neville Chamberlain also distrusted the Labor leaders and only Stanley Baldwin seems to have appreciated that the new party could be fitted comfortably into the British framework.[44]

With the formation of the first Labor cabinet in 1924 (it was really a minority government dependent on Liberal votes), ideological fears about socialism increased even more. It does not matter that the first Labor government was weak; the fact that it extended *de jure* recognition to the Soviet Union within two weeks of coming into office was enough. In the ensuing recriminations over the help the Liberals had given Labor to reach office, the Liberal party began to fall apart. Churchill and Austen Chamberlain crossed

---

[44] For Chamberlain's attitude towards Labor, see Iain Macleod, *Neville Chamberlain* (New York, 1962), pp. 119, 120, 203.

the floor of the House of Commons to the conservative side. A trade agreement signed a few months later would have given British goods favored nation treatment in the Russian market, but the treaty was opposed by Liberals and Conservatives alike. But these are mere details in a larger tableau of ideology and party politics. In 1794 the Whig party had split over the French revolution; in 1924 the Liberal party was undergoing a similar disintegration amidst ideological controversy. Henceforth His Majesty's "loyal opposition" would be the Labor party.

For the conservative leaders, whose world was forever less secure, it was an unenviable prospect. A socialist party, no matter how mild, was a standing threat to the world of privilege and property. Even if the first generation of leaders were respected amiables, what about the more outspoken of the rank and file? Also unclear in the early 1920's was the connection, if any, between the Labor party and international communism. Here conservative imagination tended to run wild with the worst fears being presented as accomplished facts. It was not uncommon in less enlightened conservative circles to refer to the Labor party as "Reds" and to equate them with communists. The Zinoviev letter is a case in point. Although addressed to the British Communist party the blame for it was immediately laid at the door of the Labor party, a wholly separate organization, which contributed to its loss of the election in November 1924. Finally, whether the letter was genuine has never been established though conservatives in the 1960's still thought so.[45]

The conservative government of Stanley Baldwin had ample time to provide a solution for Britain's post-war economic malaise. However, the orthodox financial policies of Winston Churchill, Chancellor of the Exchequer, stressed monetary rather than human needs. A stable pound sterling would assure capital for investments but left British exports at a disadvantage in world markets. A hard currency helped investors but it spelled unemployment for the workers. Quite unintentionally Churchill's traditional policies swelled the ranks of the Labor party and augmented conservative fears. Seen in perspective, the General Strike of 1926 was only an incident in the adolescence of the Labor party but a traumatic shock for the conservatives of Victorian years.[46]

It is not necessary to recall in detail the sorry record of both parties during the Depression. Voted once more into office, though without an absolute majority in the Commons, MacDonald and the Labor party were unequal to the 1931 financial crisis. Once again it was a question of monetary versus

---

[45] Macleod, *op. cit.*, p. 108.

[46] It should be emphasized that Churchill's economic policies were the standard remedy of that time; it would be misleading to put forward any class or any other theory as explanation.

human demands. Faced with a £ 170 million budget deficit, the Labor government had to cut costs which meant unemployment relief, or allow deficit financing to take its toll on the value of the pound. The economic solution of the crisis might have been predicted, but the political repercussions went far beyond the expected norm. The MacDonald cabinet, divided on the budget decision, resigned and new elections or a conservative government were expected. Instead, MacDonald was persuaded by the King to form a national coalition to handle the financial crisis. The pound was saved, the dole was cut, the conservatives controlled the cabinet and the prime minister was henceforth a politician without a party.

The crisis made a profound impression on both parties with unfortunate results. The Labor party felt betrayed by its own leaders and withdrew into a highly suspicious attitude about the opposition. Despite its debacle the party survived undivided and more concerned about its program for a better Britain. The consequences for the Conservative party were different and on the whole detrimental, but this was not understood at the time. In the first place, the conservatives had dealt with the financial dilemma in a very "starchy" manner, equating the salvation of the pound with that of the country. They were upset by the political dangers of an unstable currency and would hereafter be excessively motivated by economic principles to the exclusion of other considerations. In plain terms, the second consequence for the conservative leaders was a fixation about 1931 which made other crises elsewhere pale by comparison. Thirdly, the resolution of the government impasse through a national coalition cabinet which served as a facade for conservative control, gave the party an unsavory aspect. It was widely held that the conservatives had duped MacDonald.

The conservatives had, however, a very different view. From the standpoint of power and responsibility the Labor party had clearly failed to do its duty when the economic conditions called for drastic measures. The Laborites had "cut and run" and the Conservative party had had to rescue the ship of state. Clearly, the Labor party was not fit to govern and the conservatives were the indispensable men for the job. This was the most harmful outcome of the 1931 crisis. It blinded the Conservative party to legitimate labor opposition in domestic and foreign questions. Convinced of their vital role, the conservative leaders wrapped their policies in a moral righteousness that became unassailable. To question the wisdom of their policies was tantamount to unpatriotic behavior. Not only did this situation undermine the significance of parliamentary opposition, but later on policies could be sponsored that in ordinary times would have been questioned strenuously.

In keeping Labor out of office (and the electorate obligingly cooperated in

1931 and 1935) conservatives were sure that they had averted socialism and chaos. When the national government cut salaries and the dole there were riots in London, Liverpool, Glasgow and even a mutiny in the navy at Invergordon. What would have happened had Labor been in power no one knew, but these disturbances played strongly on ideological fears. It would take another fourteen years and a world war before the electorate would vote Labor into office again. In the intervening period fascism presented an ideological challenge of a very different sort. Its racism offered a kind of élitism that recruited only a tiny following in England, but its apparent success in overcoming the effects of the Depression through a rigidly controlled economy found somewhat more support.

Fascism's real impact, however, pointed in a different direction. After Hitler had reached power in Germany the danger of a military confrontation was quickly appreciated in London. Recognition of the problem was one thing and dealing with it was quite another. By 1934 Baldwin and Chamberlain were faced with a dilemma rather similar to William Pitt's in 1794: to meet a clear foreign danger Great Britain must mobilize her defence capabilities. Pitt failed to do so because of social and ideological considerations, but he was at war while the conservative leaders of the 1930's refused to accept the inevitability of fighting Germany. But that did not excuse them from arming Britain, if only to negotiate from strength.

Many writers since World War II have tried to demonstrate that Baldwin and Chamberlain worked earnestly at rearming Britain. If this is true, why was she so weak and unprepared in 1938–'9? Keep in mind we are discussing the defence preparations of a highly industrialized country. If experience wasn't lacking, the will to arm was. But why? Many reasons have been given, some valid and others more contrived. Public opinion was not ready, it was weary of war, it wanted friendship rather than conflict with Germany, and all this is true. This predicament has led to charges, now refuted, that Baldwin had avoided rearmament in order to win the 1935 election.

The circumstances are rather different. Baldwin and Chamberlain did in fact undertake Britain's rearmament, but at a rate that bore little relationship to her material and technological strength. The reasons for this are twofold: to rearm Britain in the 1930's at the required speed would have involved great financial sacrifices and required close cooperation and some sharing of power with labor. The first condition would cause impoverishment of the middle and upper classes, the second would return to the political center a force which had been excluded since 1931. Both consequences were unpalatable for obvious social and ideological reasons. The large expenditures needed for rapid rearmament could be borrowed, or raised with higher taxes, but either method would destroy the carefully husbanded recovery from the Depression, damage the export drive and undermine the stability of the pound. A concentrated production effort in aircraft or machine tools could only be accomplished by shifting highly skilled workers to these plants, and such measures could not be taken in peacetime without trade union cooperation. The cabinet was loath to obtain such collaboration for fear of having to pay a price.[47]

The men of 1931 would neither imperil the pound nor take the trade unions into their counsel, even for the sake of rearmament, and preferred to "tide things over." Two years alone (1934 and 1935) were spent on perfecting defence plans before any concrete steps were taken. Programs adopted in 1936 were out of date by 1938, and only in the latter year was it decided to stress fighter rather than bomber production. By then models coming off the drawing board were put in production without extensive testing. These details tell that the urgency to rearm was lacking, an urgency that could only have been imparted by the government. Even if Chamberlain hated war, believed in the efficacy of negotiations, and rejected the inevitability of war it would still fail to account fully for the inadequacy of Britain's armaments in 1939. The source of foreign policy cannot be discovered by ignoring the ideological factors entering into domestic affairs. The implications of a swift rearmament program stimulated an ideological *Angst* without which appeasement cannot be understood.

We are now face to face with two critical issues: ideology as a motive for policy and the consequent connection between ideology and appeasement. The charge that appeasement was ideologically motivated is not new. Keith Feiling denied it vigorously thirty years ago in his biography of Chamberlain.[48] That denial assumes, however, that ideological motivation is a conscious one like pain when we have tried to show that it is a fear which does not clearly surface in man's mind. Fear is nevertheless a powerful motive, a normal, human emotion which can be pointed to through circumstantial evidence. Chamberlain's biographer wrote that "not a trace can be found in his letters of an ideological motive" but he was looking for an open admission

---

[47] For the problem of the trade unions and the cabinet's reluctance, see Middlemas, *Diplomacy of Illusion*, p. 15; Feiling, *op. cit.*, pp. 315, 318. The financial strains of rearmament are mentioned in Chamberlain's notes, Feiling, *op. cit.*, p. 314. See also Ian Colvin, *The Chamberlain Cabinet* (New York, 1971), pp. 80–81, 117–118, 120–121, 220.

[48] Feiling, *op. cit.*, p. 467. The author does admit the presence of "political argument and political suspicion" in Chamberlain's letters. Can these be so easily separated from ideological motive?

when in fact politicians and prime ministers are not given to analyze their fears, even for themselves.[49]

The determined efforts in the 1790's and 1930's to preserve the structure of English society from egalitarian or socialist models were motivated by an anti-ideological stance. The forces of history and tradition evoked a Britannic élitism all its own, both against foreign enemies and domestic agitators, but it differed from fascism by upholding what existed rather than rebuilding society on outdated concepts. Assertions of pride and self-esteem are natural in response to ideological assault, but it is not spurred in a conscious sense by class motives. The defensive reaction seeks to protect the existing system with arguments of historical achievement and cultural uniqueness. Survival of the existing power structure will benefit the establishment, and specific policies may have promoted this end. But it has been demonstrated that the English régimes of the 1790's and 1930's were not very efficient in assuring this outcome. To sum up: the danger of an ideological onslaught led to the decision to resist. This choice was fairly automatic and could hardly have been otherwise in view of the distinct identity of the English nation and the foreign character of the ideological import. Survival of the existing system would benefit the establishment which had made the decision to oppose the challenge. Its ideological fear was latent but a sufficient motive in the urge to survive.

The heart of the evidence each time are the statements of England's leaders and the correlation that can be drawn with policy decisions. In the earlier period Bonaparte's coup d'état offers a clear case. His assumption of power was immediately understood as the end of the revolution and the ideological offensive. Canning, who was close to Pitt, and Sir John Macpherson who wrote Addington repeatedly, grasped the significance of the change in France.[50] Pitt's rejection of Bonaparte's first offer to negotiate was followed by peace talks within six months. While he failed Addington succeeded in making peace, but ideology as a motive for policy is closely interrelated. Peace with a revolutionary republic, which had been tried, would leave England face to face with ideological danger; peace with a general who suppressed jacobins and established one-man rule was a much safer proposition. Britain needed peace for economic and social reasons, if she could not live with high food prices, scarcity and rioting.

---

[49] *Loc. cit.* The exception must be Baldwin's speech of November 1932 in the House of Commons when he described in vivid terms the terror of warfare from the air. House of Commons Debate, Vol. 270, Fifth Series, c. 632.

[50] See Macpherson's letter to Addington, in Pellew, *op. cit.*, I, p. 246 Sir John Macpherson to the Speaker, December 18, 1799. "The reign of jacobinism in France is over..."

Peace with Bonaparte did not come cheap, as Pitt discovered. What could Addington do? Hopes had been raised so high and so often that English expectations were great and of some influence. He might disappoint these hopes and go on, but could his government survive a simultaneous onslaught of a frustrated Bonaparte? Macpherson warned Addington that to resist the First Consul's proposals would be to radicalize him with dire consequences for England.[51] The search for peace thus deteriorated into a policy of appeasement, but this quest must be seen as motivated by a double concern: for domestic unrest and for a renewed jacobinism if peace with Bonaparte proved unattainable.

In the twentieth century the existence of ideology and appeasement is readily admitted, but any connection between them is stoutly denied. Baldwin and Chamberlain distrusted communist ideology; their words leave no doubt about its dangers during the 1926 General Strike. The mild socialism of the Labor party had proved unequal to the crisis of 1931; it too had to be kept out of office if possible. Fascism, on the other hand, was no ideological threat but could become a military danger. Caught between the Great Depression and a revitalized Germany, Great Britain was forced to rearm. Could she assume the burden of a race to match Germany plane for plane? Not without wrecking the economy, impoverishing the middle and upper class and sharing power with the unions whose cooperation was essential. That was the price for a top-speed rearmament policy and Chamberlain rejected it. He preferred the turtle to the hare: rearmament at a measured pace and an alternative to conflict. We know that alternative as appeasement.

Even the concern of driving Bonaparte to jacobin extremes, if Great Britain failed to meet his terms, finds an echo in the 1930's. Hitler was seen as a "moderate" in Nazi circles, and London believed that appeasing him would prevent "extremists" like Ribbentrop from doing the worst. But, as Baldwin argued and Chamberlain considered, it might be possible to smash the Nazis with French and Russian cooperation. What then? Germany would surely fall into chaos and go communist. That consequence would be much worse than trying to meet her halfway. Here again at the source of the policy we find ideology as a contributing factor.[52] The link connecting ideology and appeasement is fear: what would become of an obsolete England? This ideological *Angst* was not just a narrow class interest but an anti-modernist reaction. In their concern for the future the traditional men governing Britain tried to ward off ideology like an evil spirit. They sought to come to terms with the

---

[51] "Addington MSS," Box 1801, Devon Record Office, Exeter, Sir John Macpherson to Henry Addington, June 17, August 14, September 2, 1801.

[52] Middlemas and Barnes, *Baldwin*, p. 918; Middlemas, *Diplomacy of Illusion*, pp. 261, 277.

new leaders on the continent, products of revolution who seemed to have tamed the rampant forces of instability and change. Perhaps it was a sensible policy for sober minds, but revolution and ideology cannot be reduced to checks and balances. The attempt to fend off ideology through appeasement was a grave miscalculation. Historical phenomena like Bonaparte or Hitler will not "stay bought" for long because their own position is too uncertain. Appeasement was no shield yet Englishmen would not see that ideology like the wind cannot be turned away.

CHAPTER V

PORTRAITS OF TWO EPOCHS

The crucial element, the irreducible factor in history is the human dimension. Without humanity, whether individual or en masse, the study of the past would properly belong to geology. Change, growth and development are dependent on many variables, all important, but inseparable from human decision-making. This emphasis on the human factor in history has been the touchstone of the theory that each historical event is unique – what some have called historicism. This theory cannot accommodate the comparative approach, while it is our contention that given certain similar historical conditions, different individuals have reacted in the same way although separated in time. From another perspective, the materialist interpretation of history has contributed much to our analysis and understanding of the past, but when it attempts to stress historical movements at the expense of individual contributions historical materialism leaves the field of objective inquiry and becomes dogma.

Thus appeasement was no puppet theater but the deliberate policy of certain key individuals. In Great Britain policy decisions are made at the highest level, by the prime minister in accordance with his cabinet, although sub-cabinet committees composed of only a few ministers may reach substantial agreement before the entire cabinet decides. Such committees can be more easily controlled by the prime minister who serves as its chairman. Certain cabinet officers like the Chancellor of the Exchequer and the Secretary of State for Foreign Affairs carry more weight with the prime minister than most other ministers. Parliament neither initiates policy nor is it responsible for implementation, all of which has been delegated to the cabinet. The power of the prime minister is enormous, exactly because it is legitimate, confirmed by majority vote and supported by a freely elected representative body. Properly speaking, the house of commons is not a legislative body at all; legislation does not originate there (except in the case of a private member's bill) but is introduced by the cabinet. The House can then examine, analyze and question the proposed bill, but eventually through various readings it can only ratify or reject the government's legislation.

The evolution in power of the British executive was gradual; it started in the eighteenth century but Pitt had certainly less authority than Baldwin. The declining influence of the crown augmented the strength of parliament's executive, and here lies the peculiar position of the modern prime minister. His power does not flow directly from the electorate but from the majority party in the house of commons of which he remains a member. As leader he effectively steers both representative and executive functions of the government, and this lack of separation between these two gives him enormous powers of initiation, acceptance and enforcement of policy. He regulates the sessions of Parliament, decides the dates of elections and adjournments, and controls the flow of information for legislative deliberations. Independent action on the part of the house of commons is possible, but it has to be taken in the teeth of executive opposition and virtually carries the stigma of censure.

With authority concentrated in this manner much depends on the make-up of the cabinet. If the prime minister is a strong figure who surrounds himself with loyal supporters rather than independent minds his government will nearly be a one-man show. This was certainly the case with Neville Chamberlain.[1] Whatever the circumstances, the decision-making process moves in a narrow circle from civil servant to minister, cabinet committee and ultimately the prime minister and his cabinet. By the time a decision is brought before the full cabinet pro and con arguments and alternatives have been explored, and the ratification expected of the ministers takes place in the restricted atmosphere of a few predetermined choices. In the case of appeasement, where the attitude of the prime minister was well known, the evaluation of policy decisions became something less than objective. Sound advice was not appreciated and experience counted for little. The Foreign Office staff was regarded as being out of touch with "reality" and unsympathetic to appeasement. Ultimately, a few close advisers supported Chamberlain's policies and the full cabinet was shut out of his confidence. The decision to appease Germany was taken deliberately, though only by very few. The support of many in Parliament and outside it followed as a matter of course. The structure of the prime minister's authority made effective opposition in the cabinet or the party nearly impossible while resignation was tantamount to political harakiri.

What is true for the actual decision, made at the highest level by the prime minister, is also the case for the extent to which that policy will be carried out. Since appeasement was not a statute with set limits the range of its application was uncertain. Only the prime minister or his intimate advisers could decide

---

[1] Keith Feiling, *The Life of Neville Chamberlain* (London, 1946), p. 305.

how far their policy should go. In the earlier period the negotiator in the field, free of the instant communication of today, might interpret his instructions liberally and act accordingly, hoping to be supported by his government later on. Even in the 1930's the British ambassador in Berlin took liberties with his government's directives which earned him several reprimands from the Foreign Secretary.[2] Yet neither Lord Cornwallis nor Sir Nevile Henderson could decide at what point appeasement had reached its outer limits – that remained for the prime minister and his perception of "political realities."

Since the chain of formulation-decision-execution is inconceivable without the prime minister, the first sketches should be of Pitt and Baldwin – two who experimented with but never fully endorsed appeasement. Pitt's historical reputation is infinitely greater than Baldwin's, despite the latter's recent rehabilitation, but they share an affinity for crypto-appeasement. Pitt's family background, education and early career are well known. The younger son of a remarkable father, he achieved office at a very tender age (Chancellor of the Exchequer at 23, Prime Minister at 24) and under difficult circumstances. Yet he possessed the right talents for the Britain of the 1780's, isolated, troubled by defeat in America and financially burdened with war debts. His carefully developed oratory impressed the House of Commons, his financial acumen (he was a disciple of Adam Smith) brought some order to the chaotic Exchequer, and his peace oriented retrenchment fostered the return of commercial prosperity. Pitt was fortunate in his relations with the Crown. George III needed a new first minister and Pitt, with astute electioneering, obtained a solid majority for his government with the election of 1784.

Pitt's abilities were unusual in an age when most statesmen were ignorant of economics and relegated administrative chores to clerks. Above all he prepared himself thoroughly for his major speeches in the Commons and he managed to retain sizable majorities in the House. He was respected for his achievements but Pitt was not a popular man in the sense of his opponent Charles Fox.[3] His age and personality did not allow him to unbend from the lofty position he had reached. His cold and aloof bearing avoided the familiarity which older men might use in personal contact with one so young. Yet he knew how to relax and make merry in the restricted social circles frequented by him.[4] This narrowness of Pitt's life holds true in different ways. He had few close friends, and two rather different individuals (Wilberforce

---

[2] Keith Eubank, *Munich* (Norman, Oklahoma, 1963), pp. 18, 56.
[3] See the revealing letter of the Duchess of Devonshire to Philip Francis, November 29, 1798, in *The Francis Letters*, by Sir Philip Francis, ed. by Beata Francis (New York, n.d.), II, pp. 437–438.
[4] John Ehrman, *The Younger Pitt. The Years of Acclaim* (New York, 1969), pp. 575–603.

and Windham) concluded that he knew little about mankind.[5] Pitt had no interests in the arts and did not believe that the state should be its patron. Of the world beyond England he knew little and had seen less, which may explain why he thought that revolutionary France could through financial means be brought to her knees.

It is a matter of some interest why Pitt's reputation has remained so high when his leadership after 1793 faltered in most respects. His first ten years in office had benefitted the country. As peacetime minister he had proved his worth; he was free from vice and venality though he drank a bit too much. But he was not without faults. His arrogance has been mentioned, he was "mercurial" and lacked staying power, and from his father Pitt had inherited the quality of being "always in the cellar or the garret."[6] These qualities taken together with his narrow focus brought Pitt to grief in the inferno of the war with France. Even before 1793 Pitt had precipitously abandoned principles if he encountered too much parliamentary opposition: his opposition to Russian expansion in 1791 is one example. The struggle with France required stern decisions and forward looking policies; instead, Pitt moved on impulse and improvisation. His wartime administration was chaotic and as the years went by the prime minister became tired and ill. But his ringing speeches in the House of Commons never failed him, even if Fox could be stinging in his replies.

In fact Pitt's talents were wasted in war except for his ability to keep the House of Commons spellbound with his eloquence. And he was fortunate in one respect which saved his reputation. He had gone to war to uphold a treaty and found himself before long the champion of a beleaguered island. This gave Pitt the chance to pose as the defender of British freedom against French aggression, and his oratorical skills assured him a place in the pantheon of English luminaries. How else can one explain the historical stature of a prime minister who could neither win the war nor negotiate peace, offered to surrender Holland and Belgium to France and earnestly undertook to bribe the Directory for a peace treaty? When he died Napoleon dominated the continent and England faced a struggle without end.

Stanley Baldwin too had spent his youth in the latter days of an elegant age and the better part of manhood in a revolutionary world. Neither family background, education or experience had prepared him for the disturbed century that would threaten his country. After a successful business career

---

[5] *The Life of William Wilberforce*, by his sons Robert Isaac and Samuel Wilberforce (London, 1838), II, pp. 92–93. *The Cambridge History of British Foreign Policy, 1783–1919*, Vol. I 1783–1815, ed. by A. W. Ward and G. P. Gooch (Cambridge, 1939), pp. 219–220.

[6] Richard Pares, *The Historian's Business and Other Essays* (Oxford, 1961), p. 126.

Baldwin entered Parliament in 1908 but did not gain cabinet rank till after World War I. He gained prominence in 1922 when he had a major hand in the withdrawal of the Conservative party from the National Coalition and the consequent resignation of Lloyd George. Within two years he became the party's leader and prime minister. Baldwin's tenure confirmed the hold of the middle class businessmen over the Conservative party; henceforth the men who knew the value of profits and trade would dictate policy to the exclusion of foreign adventures which cost money. Baldwin the conciliator, the man of peace, retrenchment and inertia was the perfect symbol for this hard-nosed attitude about foreign affairs.

If Baldwin the man remains somewhat of an enigma, it is because his nervous temperament hid his intentions effectively. His views of leadership were the exact opposite of Lloyd George's whose dynamic tenure of office he regarded as a dangerous force. Born in Wales Baldwin was an Englishman in style, although he retained something of the Welsh fluency if he wished to spellbind his listeners. His lassitude was part affectation and part innate for he strongly believed that England needed quiet leadership and social peace. "When the world war ended," he said, "we were in a new world ... class conscious and revolutionary..."[7] His prescription was to preach reconciliation and it must be said that Baldwin contributed more to preserving the fabric of British society than he has been given credit for. Churchill called him a mild socialist.[8] Baldwin treated the Labor party leaders with respect as His Majesty's loyal opposition. But Baldwin had other qualities as well which may explain his success as a politician.

His career in the iron business was the preparation for his role as party leader. Baldwin did not believe in forceful action, direct challenges or confrontations. The quiet chat, the appeal to one's sense of decency and the passage of time were his stock in trade. As party leader he did not make enemies and he mollified his opponents. His solid rusticity made him the perfect spokesman for an age when Englishmen only wanted to enjoy what was theirs, and they were ready (in large numbers as the elections proved) to accept his slogan "you know you can trust me." Baldwin's avuncular appearance, his preference for English habits and traditions and his appeal for moderation precluded the ideological divisions which he feared so much. For a generation which wanted only to be left alone he was the genial politician.

Of course he enjoyed power and with the crises of 1926 and 1931 he may have convinced himself, as he did others, that he was the indispensable man.

---

[7] As quoted in Thomas Jones, *A Diary with Letters, 1931–1950* (London, 1954), p. 204.

[8] Winston S. Churchill, *The Gathering Storm* (Boston, 1948), p. 21.

Although not without his critics in the Conservative party no one could muster the following to oust him. Despite his success with the voters Baldwin cannot be called a strong prime minister: in 1926 the General Strike was settled by others while the government tried to carry on; in 1931 George V played a larger role than Baldwin,[9] and only in 1936 did the prime minister assert himself on the moral issue of the King and Mrs. Simpson. It is with this debatable performance in mind that we search for Baldwin the statesman beyond his record as a prime minister of retrenchment. Would he who had failed to provide leadership in 1926 adopt a firm line against Hitler in 1936? Recent attempts to rehabilitate Baldwin have refurbished the record of his domestic policies and emphasized his conciliatory role. Similarly, he has been absolved of the charge that he avoided rearmament in order to win the 1935 election.[10]

Baldwin's contribution to foreign affairs and rearmament remains a matter of debate. His English insularity failed to help him; despite annual visits to Aix-les-Bains he did not once visit the League of Nations which was nearby. Foreign relations seemed to bore him, or perhaps because he felt uncertain and remembered unpleasant experiences (with Poincaré) the subject drove him more into a shell. He resisted meeting Hitler and told Eden to keep England out of all involvement with the Spanish civil war. In the mounting crisis of the Nazi revolution Baldwin watched, waited and hoped for time to solve the danger. He permitted the first hesitant steps on the road to rearmament, but it cannot be said that the required urgency was evident in his administration. Baldwin discouraged any French initiatives over Germany's remilitarization of the Rhineland; we know that he hoped that Hitler would turn eastward and come to blows with Stalin.[11] But this was only a wish; Baldwin had neither plans nor policy for the future. His languor irritated the Chancellor of the Exchequer who was anxious to take charge and direct an active foreign policy.

The efforts to restore Baldwin's image cannot pretend that he was a great prime minister. As a leader in times of great stress his nerves failed him, as he himself admitted, and yet a curious benefit resulted from this inactivity. In foreign affairs he avoided commitments or policies leading to disastrous consequences; this inactivity is not policy but it prevents mistakes. The

---

[9] Baldwin in fact went back to his vacation spot at Aix, leaving matters in the hands of Neville Chamberlain. Feiling, *op. cit.*, p. 190.

[10] Keith Middlemas and John Barnes, *Baldwin. A Biography* (New York, 1970), *passim*. R. Bassett, "Telling the truth to the people: the myth of the Baldwin 'Confession'," *The Cambridge Journal*, II (November 1948), pp. 84–95.

[11] Middlemas and Barnes, *op. cit.*, pp. 947, 955, 1025.

Baldwin cabinet did not object to appeasement, either of Mussolini or Hitler, but would not proceed to pursue it actively as a policy. When it did in Abyssinia's case it failed disastrously. Appeasement at this stage was reconciliation without concessions, to avoid antagonizing Hitler and treat him as a respectable statesman. The climax of this rapprochement came in 1936 with the Anglo-German naval agreement.

In comparing the crypto-appeasement of Pitt and Baldwin differences as well as similarities become obvious. Pitt conducted a major war haphazardly, Baldwin lived through a world war while holding a minor post. As prime ministers both men tried to negotiate with major continental adversaries without seeming to be too conceding in the attempt. Their efforts seemed forever to be close to success and yet no nearer; it was a cat-and-mouse game with the obvious danger of getting too close to the cat. Neither Pitt nor Baldwin hazarded that chance. In due time each left office with the great struggle unresolved and their country still facing a fight for its survival. Only caution had restrained them from outright appeasement.

If their search for peace had been tempered by many considerations, their respective successors – Henry Addington and Neville Chamberlain – were less restrained in the pursuit of an agreement. These were the men who dared to choose peace despite the risks and lost in the eyes of history.

Henry Addington had entered politics in the accepted eighteenth century fashion: a patron – in this case William Pitt – had secured him a seat in the House of Commons. His father had been a physician. In the aristocratic society of eighteenth century England a physician was little better than a barber and an object of ridicule. But Addington *père* was apparently a very fine physician with the right contacts: the elder Pitt was his patient. He was also innovative in the treatment of the mentally deranged – a talent which did not go unrewarded in the reign of George III. The son would remember his father's remedies and as prime minister recommend them with success to the King's doctors.[12]

It was not unusual for middle class talent to reach the House of Commons; a contemporary figure of even humbler beginnings – George Canning – would rival Addington in reaching the top, but he was of far different temperament. Still, Addington was probably the first modern prime minister of middle class origins. His career was truly launched when in 1789 Pitt nominated him for Speaker of the House and he was elected at the age of thirty two. He was so far an acceptable nonentity, but Pitt knew him to be a careful student of par-

[12] The best biography of Addington is Philip Ziegler, *Addington. A Life of Henry Addington, First Viscount Sidmouth* (New York, 1963).

liamentary procedure. As Speaker of the House of Commons Addington served with distinction and earned respect for his person and for the position he occupied. He possessed the right qualities to be heard and obeyed. Although unspectacular in temperament and as an orator, Addington had a sound if somewhat ponderous intelligence. His rulings were fair, however, and his behavior was exemplary. In a word, as a Speaker he was a great success and he would no doubt have been satisfied to end his career in the chair. Only when he resorted to his father's wisdom and harangued the House on the greater nutritive value of bran over grain did he become an object of merriment with the nickname of "the Doctor."[13]

Pitt did not share this view. He saw the Speaker as a valuable political ally. In 1793 he had asked Addington to take Dundas' place as Secretary of State but the offer was declined. More significant perhaps were the events of the year of disasters – 1797 – when Pitt considered resignation and suggested that the Speaker succeed him.[14] When this took place four years later it was the occasion for a great deal of hilarity, but the fact is that the King and Pitt believed the choice to be logical. Whether Addington was prepared to be prime minister and suited for the office is another matter. He had not sought the post and only accepted it after special pleading by the King. Pitt had not trained the Speaker to be his successor, although Addington was part of a small circle which was taken into the prime minister's confidence. His administrative experience was slight but more serious was the attitude which greeted Addington as the new prime minister. He was treated simultaneously as usurper and fop, a man who would not last a month.[15]

One serious consequence was the unwillingness of talented men to join the new administration. In her usual outspoken fashion Lady Holland described the cabinet as being "formed out of the dregs of the old one."[16] It is true that Pitt was a difficult act to follow and Addington deserves credit for taking on an almost impossible task. Only a man of courage and stamina would seek to govern a country whose King had again lost his reason, where food shortages and riots grew worse day by day and whose enemies had formed a league to drive her off the sea. It would take the utmost care in husbanding her resources to survive; luckily, Addington was a competent administrator who

---

[13] This was in 1800 when food shortages were severe. Ziegler, *op. cit.*, p. 75.

[14] *Ibid.*, pp. 71, 81.

[15] In this "Upstairs-Downstairs" age, readers might enjoy one contemporary observation about the new government. "This Administration is as if the footmen were called up to the second [i.e., servants'] table" said someone to Lady Glenbervie. *The Diaries of Sylvester Douglas, Lord Glenbervie*, ed. by Francis Bickley (London, 1928), I, p. 169, February 14, 1801.

[16] *The Journal of Elizabeth Lady Holland (1791–1811)*, ed. by the Earl of Ilchester (New York, 1908), II, p. 129, February 11, 1801.

improved tax collections and food distribution. Despite these advances, or
the military victories in the Baltic and Egypt, the desire for peace was
uppermost in man's mind. In the words of Lady Holland: "the first laugh
over, people begin to think this Administration may last, and if they com-
mence negotiation they will even become popular."[17]

Addington was no fool and had more sense than Pitt in knowing what the
country needed. He was also less concerned about his political reputation and
dignity than his predecessor. The new prime minister was devoid of Pitt's
arrogance and less bound by commitments and precedents; in brief, he was a
simpler man free to take a new tack. The negotiations which he opened
shortly need not concern us here, but rather that he announced his firm
intention towards peace in his first statement as prime minister to the House.
Moreover, he declared "that no consideration, arising from the form of
government in France would on their [i.e., British] part, obstruct negotiation
... The question must be one of terms, and of terms only."[18] He remained
faithful to this declaration but did not realize that the other side felt no similar
compulsion for peace.

The preliminary peace agreement brought the government much acclaim
and the prime minister the popularity which had seemed impossible eight
months before. Addington had achieved what had eluded Pitt since 1795:
peace on terms that "were as good as, under all the circumstances of our
situation, could have been expected."[19] Since Parliament approved the preliminary articles and the final treaty with overwhelming majorities, Addington dissolved the House and called for new elections in June, 1802. That
summer his reputation stood higher than it would ever be again, and it is
therefore not surprising that the complacent and self-satisfied facets of his
character appear more prominent. The prime minister was after all a man of
limited vision and experience and his success brought his vain, even opinionated temperament into the open. He felt sure about the trust he had
placed in Bonaparte and gravely informed the House that "no encouragement should be given to any persons, whatever their character might be, to
subvert the present government of France.[20] And furthermore:

---

[17] *Ibid.*, II, p. 130, February 26, 1801.

[18] As quoted in George Pellew, *The Life and Correspondence of the Right Honble Henry
Addington, First Viscount Sidmouth* (London, 1847), I, p. 361, March 25, 1801.

[19] According to the Foreign Secretary, Lord Hawkesbury, discussing the terms of the Amiens
treaty of 1802. *The Parliamentary History of England from the Earliest Period to the Year 1803*
(London, 1820), XXXVI, p. 768, May 13, 1802.

[20] *Ibid.*, XXXVI, p. 85, November 3, 1801.

I know of nothing in the disposition of the government of France, nor in the disposition of the person at the head of the government of France, that warrants any apprehension that the peace now concluded may not be lasting.[21]

Perhaps we can excuse Addington for his short-sightedness; Pitt admitted to Lord Malmesbury that for a time he had held similar views.[22] But in matters of military preparedness, the continuation of certain taxes and the promotion of trade the prime minister was careless and overconfident. Bonaparte's "record" was not good and the best guarantee against duplicity was military strength. Instead, Addington cut the budget for military expenditures, reduced the fleet, put officers on half pay and ended the heaviest taxes. Napoleon resisted a trade agreement with England and its goods were kept out of European markets for the sake of French commercial interests. Nothing Addington said or did ruined his reputation with the City as quickly as the failure of his commercial policies. Still, the peace was popular and Englishmen flocked to see the new Paris and the First Consul. Canning's gibes could not alter the taste for Addington and his "mediocracy" – only Bonaparte's policies would accomplish that.

So long as peace reigned Addington could rule despite the parliamentary cabals. He remained a favorite of the King and received Pitt's support in diminishing measure. For George III talking with Addington was like thinking out loud, but Pitt resented his successor's vanity and budget cuts. The renewal of war over Malta, which the British refused to evacuate in 1803, ended the *raison d'être* of the Addington cabinet. A prime minister of peace cannot become a war leader overnight and though he tried Addington retained his office for only another year. His military administration was probably not inferior to Pitt's but he utterly lacked the latter's eloquence. With Canning in the van chipping away, Addington's parliamentary support gradually eroded until his majority fell below forty in an overwhelmingly Conservative House of Commons. At that point he resigned (April 30, 1804), never again to be prime minister but with a long ministerial career at the Home Office still ahead of him. He had served his country at a time of great distress, but it was his misfortune to have had to match wits with one of history's strongest personalities.

If Addington seems remote and a little ridiculous to us now, the image the world retains of Neville Chamberlain has far stronger contrasts. He has become the symbol of an age, the embodiment of a political concept. Beginning with Keith Feiling many writers have tried to picture a wiser and

---

[21] *Ibid.*, XXXVI, p. 816, May 14, 1802.

[22] *Diaries and Correspondence of James Harris, First Earl of Malmesbury*, ed. by his grandson, the third Earl (London, 1845), IV, p. 67, April 8, 1802.

more deliberate Chamberlain than caught the public eye; we certainly know a good deal more about his policies than his immediate contemporaries. There are only two biographies of him and a third is in preparation.[23] The public view of Chamberlain was formal and strictly business-like; casual banter and easy informality were beyond him. He had none of the bonhomie of a Churchill, the countrified airs of a Baldwin or the easy charm of Lloyd George. If the first impression of him is an unsympathetic one subsequent biographers have done little to soften this picture.[24]

This should be less cause for surprise if one keeps in mind that Chamberlain was an exceedingly diligent man, a virtual workhorse with a compulsion for details and a reluctance to delegate work. By making himself indispensable to the Conservative party, and later doing the same in Baldwin's cabinet, he reached the position of the indisputable successor. Churchill as Chancellor of the Exchequer had a much better claim in 1929, but he broke with Baldwin in 1931 over the India question and resigned from the shadow cabinet. He did not take part in the discussions with the Labor government that summer about the financial crisis. Chamberlain, on the other hand, had taken charge of the party organization after 1929, stood by Baldwin in 1931 when his resignation was suggested from several sides, and was at the center of the crisis discussions which led to the National government. His reward was to be one of only four Conservative ministers in the new cabinet. After the Conservative electoral victory in October Chamberlain became Chancellor of the Exchequer. Churchill, opposed to the India bill and protection, was excluded from the National government.

This upturn in Chamberlain's career came late in life: he was 62 in 1931. Nothing so far had indicated that he might qualify to be prime minister. He had entered the House of Commons after World War I. Until then his career had been made in the municipal affairs of Birmingham. With his attention to detail he made his mark in committee work at Westminster, and in 1922 joined Bonar Law's cabinet. After short stints as Postmaster General, Minister of Health and even Chancellor of the Exchequer, Chamberlain settled in as the Health Minister in Baldwin's cabinet. Since housing was part of his responsibility, and he had gained much experience about it in Birmingham, Chamberlain was well suited for this ministerial post. As Minister of Health Chamberlain left a very constructive record; his origins (non-conformist), family tradition (service to the community), and party principles (Tory paternalism) were a distinct advantage to him. In the cabinet he was cooper-

[23] Keith Feiling (1946), Iain Macleod (1962) and David Dilks' is yet to appear.
[24] According to Harold Nicolson Chamberlain had "the manner of a clothes-brush," Harold Nicolson, *Diaries and Letters, 1930–1939*, Vol. I (New York, 1966), p. 345, June 6, 1938.

ative and got along well with Baldwin and Churchill, whose spectacular manners were far removed from his own down-to-earth style. As a debater he was forceful rather than eloquent, withering in criticism and perhaps too quick to take offense at opposition. Since by sheer hard work he had mastered his subjects in detail he did not suffer fools gladly. All in all, Chamberlain was a formidable administrator.

Did he have the political instincts, however, to reach for the "top of the greasy pole"? We know that as second son of a brilliant father he had been overshadowed by parent and older brother. His determination to succeed had not been dampened by it, but his disposition and temper had been affected. He arrived late in life at his objectives: marriage, political career, and as head of the government when he was nearing seventy. He had known the bitter taste of adversity but it only made him work harder. This characteristic, coupled with level-headedness and a sober view of life were the qualities which made him useful to Baldwin and the Conservative party. The rise of Neville Chamberlain is indeed one of constant administrative effort, in business, parliament, minister of health, party manager and finally as a successful Chancellor of the Exchequer during the depression. Here lies the key to Chamberlain's achievements and his limitations. He could rescue, improve and manage an organizational structure, but he was far less adept in his relationships with individuals.

There was nothing underhanded about Chamberlain's rise in the Conservative hierarchy. After the election of 1929 he moved into a managerial vacuum, pulling both party and leadership together, supporting Baldwin and finally gaining office again – this time as Chancellor of the Exchequer. It was to be his best performance in the bleak years of the depression. By 1935 the worst of the crisis was past and not a little of the recovery was due to Chamberlain's management of Britain's resources. The Baldwin-Chamberlain team supplied the right ingredients: Baldwin's avuncular manner screened Chamberlain's tough policies while the latter's steady determination braced the prime minister's weak nerves. In 1931 Chamberlain's chances as successor were by no means clear, but his achievements as Chancellor and influence in the cabinet had by 1935 all but settled the matter. Whether Baldwin wanted it that way is not clear; however, his Chancellor's driving ways had left him little choice, especially since Chamberlain now also occupied a most influential position in the Conservative party. Will power had sustained his career, efficiency had made him indispensable to the party and later to the government; now he was to step on the rung where neither his father nor brother could reach.

Chamberlain had earned his reputation in domestic politics, but it is untrue, as has so often been asserted, that he lacked experience in foreign affairs. He had travelled extensively abroad, visited Germany, lived in the Bahamas, negotiated with foreign statesmen at the Lausanne conference of 1932 to end reparations, and predicted the advent of Hitler more than a year before it occurred.[25] In 1934 Chamberlain tried to prevent a German-Japanese alliance, which could spell disaster for the British empire in the Far East, by sponsoring an Anglo-Japanese agreement. This was two years before the Anti-Comintern Pact. The plan foundered on the rock of American opposition, but this was not the fault of "an earnest and opinionated pro-vincial" as Vansittart called Chamberlain.[26] Churchill, MacDonald and Halifax had at one time or another all suggested that Chamberlain be made Foreign Secretary and only the latter's opposition had prevented it. "I should loathe and detest the social ceremonies..." he decided and rejected the expense of the office. As always his parsimony in emotion and imagination prevailed.[27]

His shortcomings were in the way he approached foreign affairs, as if these were another extension of domestic politics. Chamberlain expected his prag-matism, once properly explained, to be convincing to all reasonable men. He detested war as a horrible waste and resented the costs of rearmament. Hitler was not completely sane – that much the prime minister knew – but he too must want to avoid the holocaust of another world war. It did not occur to Chamberlain – he could not conceive it – that the Führer longed for war. Under the circumstances pragmatism was worse than useless; it was po-sitively dangerous. Secondly, Chamberlain was inflexible as a result of the many struggles he had waged in the course of his career. He might listen to different advisers, but once he had determined which line he would take nothing could alter his decision. In foreign policy it is advisable to keep one's options open, but this approach had no appeal for the prime minister who believed that success could only result from straight and narrow paths leading to clear objectives. But worst of all was Chamberlain's obsession about failure. Once again he had staked his reputation, as in the Bahamas when a young man or in the world war as Minister of National Service. The prime minister's insistent search for an understanding with Germany must be seen in terms of his individual compulsion. The absolute need to succeed reduced

[25] Feiling, *op. cit.*, p. 201. It is equally untrue that Chamberlain had never flown in an airplane before he went to visit Hitler. *Ibid.*, p. 104.

[26] D. C. Watt, *Personalities and Policies. Studies in the Formulation of British Foreign Policy in the Twentieth Century* (South Bend, 1965), pp. 83–99. Vansittart as quoted in Macleod, *op. cit.*, p. 179.

[27] Macleod, *op. cit.*, p. 179.

appeasement to a personal quest and made him sweep aside the most valid objections. Yet foreign affairs can be like quicksand and the efficient way towards "a reasonable understanding" may lead into disaster.[28]

There is no further need to dwell on this or the debacle of his policies. Some of his contemporaries realized the futility of appeasement yet withheld their criticism from the prime minister. It was nearly impossible to resist Chamberlain's arguments in favor of peace: they were popular, made sense and had the right moral tone. Addington had had a similar advantage when he strove to make peace with Bonaparte. The support each received for his peace offensive gave him boundless confidence and encouraged their opinionated views. The desire for peace is commendable, even noble, but its emotional impact can affect the most level-headed person. It will forever remain a question whether Chamberlain's "peace with honour . . . peace for our time" and Addington's "this is not an ordinary peace, it is a reconciliation. . . ." were spoken as an emotional reaction to the tide of popular hysteria.[29] But this mood did not last. Their momentous decisions had been taken in the face of much discouraging news; only their lack of insight in foreign affairs had seen them through as if to confound the specialists. Soon, however, their respective opponents gave ample evidence that peace with them would be an ephemeral experience.

The further aggression of Bonaparte in Italy and of Hitler against Czechoslovakia served to dispel any illusions that might have sustained Addington or Chamberlain. The collapse of their peace policies was as spectacular as its initial reception. Had either Addington or Chamberlain possessed a lively imagination they might have avoided what happened after Amiens and Munich. But both men were limited by background and training, unable to suspect the worst and lacking in the capacity to speculate about the mentality of their opponents. Nothing in their English middle class origins had prepared them to anticipate the deceit and treachery that was the stock in trade of the revolutionary adventurer. They were not alone in misjudging Bonaparte or Hitler, but one cannot excuse prime ministers if they lack foresight.[30] At most we can fault the system that allows men of such caliber to reach the highest office in the land.

For external affairs the Foreign Secretary is the eyes and ears of the cabinet,

---

[28] Feiling, *op. cit.*, p. 324.

[29] Eubank, *op. cit.*, p. 227: *Letters of Admiral of the Fleet, The Earl of St. Vincent*, ed. by David B. Smith (London, 1922), I, p. 283.

[30] Even after the outbreak of war in 1939, Chamberlain still believed that Hitler had been sincere at Munich: "he had really meant what he signed and said; but he had changed his mind later." See John R. Colville, *Man of Valour. The Life of Field-Marshal The Viscount Gort* (London, 1972), p. 118. Chamberlain made this declaration to the author of this biography.

but his influence depends on the role of the prime minister. If the latter has no interests in foreign matters the secretary can assume the major share in the formulation of policy, but the times this has happened are rare. The circumstances of Addington's appointment – the result of a crisis of confidence between the cabinet and the King, and the burden of an unsuccessful war – required that the prime minister take the lead in foreign affairs. His foreign secretary, Lord Hawkesbury, was only thirty one years old, without experience or qualification, except as the son of one of George III's major political lieutenants – Charles Jenkinson, first Earl of Liverpool. After the languor of Stanley Baldwin Neville Chamberlain appeared as a masterful personality, and he took from the first a direct hand in the conduct of foreign relations. Within a year he had replaced one foreign secretary and appointed Lord Halifax as the new foreign expert in the cabinet. His skill as Indian Viceroy in negotiating with Ghandi may in Chamberlain's mind have qualified him equally for dealing with Hitler.

Even if foreign secretaries were secondary figures in the formulation of appeasement, their role in support of the government's policy was most important. It is inconceivable that the appeasement of Hitler or Bonaparte could have taken place if the foreign secretary had resisted it. A quick sketch of Hawkesbury and Halifax seems called for, if only to discover what sort of men would work with Addington or Chamberlain.

Charles Jenkinson, Lord Hawkesbury and later second Earl of Liverpool had entered Parliament in 1790 after the customary grand tour of the continent. By coincidence he was in Paris on July 14, 1789 and personally witnessed the destruction of the Bastille. Another trip in 1792 through Belgium and Germany brought home the problems of coalition warfare when he learned of the quarrels between Prussia and Austria over the war against France. His maiden speech was delivered in the House of Commons in 1792. It included an extensive review of European affairs and predicted that "the strength and influence of France are at an end, so that we may have no further danger to apprehend from that once formidable rival."[31] Hawkesbury was certainly not alone in misjudging the situation, but he fared hardly better some months later when in the wake of the British retreat from Dunkirk he advocated a quick cavalry advance to Paris as a way to end the war. The young member became the subject of much banter in the House.[32]

It was easy to poke fun at Hawkesbury's expense since he was awkward in appearance. His neck was supposedly the longest in Europe; he also suffered

[31] As quoted in Sir Charles Petrie, Bt., *Lord Liverpool and his times* (London, 1954), p. 18.
[32] *Memoirs of the Public Life and Administration of the Right Honourable the Earl of Liverpool* (London, 1827), pp. 80–81, 83.

from a twitching eyelid but the worst was his facial expression during par-liamentary debate. According to the satirists he looked "as if he had been on the rack three times and saw the wheel preparing for a fourth..."[33] All trivialities aside, young Jenkinson was made master of the mint in 1799 and to the surprise of London became Addington's foreign secretary two years later. Jenkinson *père* had worked hard to achieve high office for his son and contributed much to his character. What Hawkesbury lacked in imagination he made up by diligence and perseverance, and since his father had taught him these virtues he was fond of quoting him in his speeches. In political outlook he was strongly conservative and assigned the country gentry the most important place in society and government. Yet some aspects of his character saved him from being a prig. A Christ Church classmate described "the benignity of his personal intercourse" and observed that his "temper was extremely conciliatory."[34] He was soon to have the opportunity to exercise this trait in his contacts with Bonaparte.

It was of course Addington who ordered Hawkesbury to open conversation with M. Otto, the French commissioner for the exchange of war prisoners, who was then residing in London. The details need not concern us; what matters is that direction remained firmly in the prime minister's hands. Through the spring and summer months Hawkesbury and Otto hammered out the details of the preliminary accord. Addington had received some preliminary drafts from Lord Grenville and the advice of Pitt, but Hawkesbury's patience and accommodating temperament contributed much to the successful completion of the talks. Later on he would be fiercely criticized by William Cobbett who berated him for so lowering the dignity of his office as to negotiate with a mere "commissary of prisoners."[35] Even before this Cobbett had charged that "Otto ... must have discovered in you [Hawkesbury], during the course of the negotiation, strong symptoms of an amiable symplicity."[36] His parting shot was close to the mark: "...as a peacemaker you are rather of the lamest, but you are an excellent hand at a truce..."[37] From Windsor Castle came a different complaint; George III criticized the Foreign Secretary for having "...no head for business, no method, no punctuality."[38]

[33] Petrie, *op. cit.*, p. 15.

[34] W. R. Brock, *Lord Liverpool and Liberal Toryism, 1820 to 1827* (Cambridge, 1941), pp. 4, 6.

[35] [William Cobbett], "To the Rt. Hon. Lord Hawkesbury," *Cobbett's Weekly Political Register*, April 17, 1802, p. 399.

[36] William Cobbett, *Letters to the Right Honourable Lord Hawkesbury and to the Right Honourable Henry Addington on the Peace with Buonaparte*, 2nd ed. (London, 1802), Letter IV to Lord Hawkesbury, October 19, 1801, p. 46.

[37] *Ibid.*, Letter IX to Lord Hawkesbury, November 4, 1801, p. 142.

[38] *Malmesbury Diaries*, IV, p. 66, November, 1801.

Neither George III nor Cobbett (at this stage of his life) favored an agreement with France, so their criticism of Hawkesbury must be seen in those terms. Hawkesbury was no Fox whom even Pitt acknowledged to be the best qualified for the Foreign Office, but he wasn't a fool either. Bonaparte's proposal for an immediate naval armistice, which would have saved the French troops in Egypt, was rejected out of hand by the Foreign Secretary who remembered all too well the First Consul's methods after the armistice at Rivoli four years before. Patience and endurance are perhaps not sparkling qualities, but only these virtues carried Hawkesbury through the preliminaries to the final peace treaty. Much of his attitude is summed up in his remark: "the experiment of peace was at least as wise as the experiment of war."[39] For Hawkesbury a part of that experiment was the expectation that France had abandoned her revolutionary ways and was returning to traditions of religion and civil stability.[40] Perhaps she was but how could he be sure? He had accepted a peace treaty without commercial clauses in the hope that France could be persuaded later to agree to a mercantile pact. Meanwhile, he kept an eye on domestic demands as well as Bonaparte's ambitions.

He was to be disappointed of course, like so many, by the First Consul. Despite his failure we can see Hawkesbury's contribution more clearly now. If he had been as inflexible as Grenville England would not have had peace, and peace was needed. His experience was small but so probably was his influence. He was accommodating, he served his prime minister loyally, and above all the limited glory of making peace with Bonaparte did not exclude him from high office later on.

If the disgrace of the Amiens agreement seems not to have damaged the career of Lord Hawkesbury, the odium of the Munich pact hardly touched the life of Lord Halifax at all. He remained foreign secretary in Churchill's cabinet till January 1941 and then served five years in Washington as British ambassador. In 1944 he was created Earl of Halifax after inheriting the title of Viscount from his father. Unlike Hawkesbury Halifax was neither inexperienced nor young when chosen to be foreign secretary in Chamberlain's cabinet. Edward Wood, Baron Irwin and eventually Viscount Halifax had read history at Oxford and served in a variety of positions since 1921. He had been President of the Board of Education, Viceroy of India, Secretary of State for War and Lord President of the Council with special assignments in foreign affairs. Apparently he was a man who could fit in many slots without necessarily leaving his personal imprint on any of them.

---

[39] As quoted in *Memoirs of the Public Life*, p. 174.
[40] *Parliamentary History*, XXXVI, p. 767, May 13, 1802.

It is difficult to engage Halifax's character for an explanation. Words like aloof, vague, sceptical have been used to describe him, and others have emphasized his deeply religious feeling, high moral character and love for the Yorkshire moors. It is true that he did not wish to be foreign secretary, that immediately after Munich he advised Chamberlain to form a truly National government, including Labor, and that with the occupation of Prague he nudged Chamberlain into a stronger foreign policy against Hitler. Yet he accepted office after Eden's resignation, the prime minister ignored his suggestion about broadening the cabinet, and Chamberlain reverted to a secret appeasement of Germany in the summer months of 1939. What sort of man would continue to be part of a government whose policies conflicted with his moral principles? However, we cannot be certain that Halifax ever reached such a personal impasse.

There was in Halifax a strong disposition to be accommodating, springing from a tendency to fatalism. In the sunset of the British empire Halifax appears as the symbol of its cautious retreat. His calm detachment signified not only self-control but an aloofness that could blunder through sheer ignorance: the incident when he mistook Hitler for a footman and nearly handed him his hat is a case in point. Securely established as he was he did not seek fame or power but did well enough when asked to take on responsibility, gamely shouldering the burdens, neither discouraged nor inspired. Only the danger of another war moved him to call on Ribbentrop in May, 1938 to avoid this catastrophe that would lead to "the destruction of European civilization."[41] After it was over Halifax described Munich as "a horrible and wretched business, but the lesser of two evils."[42] One wonders how European civilization could live with the lesser evil.

Did Halifax have a foreign policy conception of his own? Professor Northedge does not think so, and one is tempted to describe his approach as careful drifting.[43] Almost two weeks after Munich Halifax had tea with the American ambassador, Joseph Kennedy. If the latter is to be believed, the Foreign Secretary had virtually surrendered the continent to Germany. It was pointless to fight Hitler, said Halifax, unless he attacked Britain or the Dominions. England must increase her air power to prevent an assault.

[41] Eubank, *op. cit.*, p. 65.

[42] The Earl of Birkenhead, *Halifax. The Life of Lord Halifax* (London, 1965), p. 407. The author concedes that Halifax had "a certain sluggishness of imagination." *Ibid.*, p. 607.

[43] F. S. Northedge, *The Troubled Giant. Britain among the Great Powers, 1916–1939* (New York, 1967), p. 489.

...after that . . . let Hitler go ahead and do what he likes in Central Europe. In other words, there is no question in Halifax's mind that reasonably soon Hitler will make a start for Danzig, with Polish concurrence, and then for Memel, with Lithuanian acquiescence, and even if he decides to go into Rumania it is Halifax's idea that England should mind her own business.[44]

When Bonaparte in violation of the treaty of Lunéville gobbled up northern Italy and infringed the neutrality of Switzerland, Hawkesbury was outraged but failed to protest because it would have been useless. Halifax seems to have done one better by anticipating Hitler and accepting the inevitable as "natural."

Despite his experience as negotiator in India, administrator in London or visitor to Hitler, Halifax remained parochial. Britain for him was closer to the Dominions than to Europe. He lacked a forceful personality or a formulated foreign policy, but relied pragmatically on events to take their turn. To that extent he compares unfavorably with Hawkesbury who, far younger and less experienced, had to learn foreign relations as he was conducting them. But neither man was a leading figure. If Halifax had political influence he was reluctant to use it against Chamberlain, while Hawkesbury listened to his father as much as to Addington. It may not be too much to say that each owed his position to the fact that he had an accommodating disposition and would not constitute a political counterweight to his chief.

Even those who merely carry out policies formulated elsewhere have a chance to influence them. This was especially true in previous times when communications were not as instant as today; the ambassador or negotiator on the spot was not a puppet at the end of a wire. While the Munich pact was the personal handiwork of Chamberlain, the Amiens treaty was negotiated by a special envoy, Charles Marquis Cornwallis. Earlier James Harris, Earl of Malmesbury had twice travelled to France in search of a peace agreement. No comparable figures in the field arose during the 1930's when prime ministers kept a tighter rein on affairs, but Sir Nevile Henderson, British ambassador to Germany, is the best approximation of the local representative working for an understanding with the new forces. A thumbnail sketch of each man is the logical extension of our portraits of two epochs.

James Harris, first Earl of Malmesbury, was one of the most accomplished English diplomats at the end of the eighteenth century. He had served in three important capitals – Madrid, St. Petersburg and The Hague – and was

---

[44] *Foreign Relations of the United States, 1938*, I, pp. 85–86, as quoted in Christopher Thorne, *The Approach of War, 1938–39* (New York, 1968), pp. 93–94. This conversation took place on October 12, 1938. Lord Halifax had already written to the British ambassador in Paris that German expansion in Central Europe was "a normal and natural thing." *Loc. cit.*

especially successful in maintaining Britain's influence on the continent despite the first League of Armed Neutrality. His efforts to keep the Czarina Catherine from being too friendly with France was liberally supported with secret service money. The markedly anti-French policies of the British government during these years of the American war for independence were continued by James Harris during his service in The Hague. A republican party overthrew the regime of the Stadholder in 1787; Malmesbury managed to counter this pro-French turn of events by having Prussian troops restore the Prince of Orange. Thus Harris at the important points of his career had been associated with anti-French policies, and his attitudes had matured accordingly. His health was not good which led to interruptions of his tours abroad, and partial deafness forced his retirement from active diplomacy after 1797.

Harris came from Salisbury where his father was a county magistrate and political figure of some importance. James had received his education at Winchester, Oxford and Leiden. Although a personal friend of Fox, he withdrew from the Whig party in 1793 and became closely allied with Pitt. In later life his mane of white hair earned him the nickname "the white lion." Malmesbury was a man of charming manner and very persuasive tongue. His political influence after his retirement went well beyond what his diaries indicate; both Canning and Lord Palmerston, who was his ward, obtained much of their politics and foreign policy from him. It was logical for Pitt to select so eminent a diplomat for the delicate task of negotiating peace with the French republicans, but it was a serious blunder. After Malmesbury had failed in 1796, and Pitt ventured to send him again for a second try, even the French expressed their disappointment that the British would not send another man.[45]

Setting aside the political turmoil in Paris, or the divisions in Pitt's cabinet, Harris was simply not the right person to negotiate peace. His anti-French turn of mind was well known; moreover, the turbulence of revolutionary politics was unsuitable for the traditional practitioner of diplomacy. It was natural for Malmesbury to work for England's interests, but his attitude of indignation over the republican system and his conviction about the superiority of the British cause made negotiations very difficult. As a diplomat who represented His Britannic Majesty Malmesbury knew what was owing to him in ceremonies and courtesies, all of which were out of style in republican Paris. No doubt the worst assault was the republic's request that the English

---

[45] Lord Granville Leveson Gower, *Private Correspondence, 1781–1821* (London, 1917), I, p. 156, GLG to his mother, June 24, 1797.

King surrender the title King of France, meaningless since the fifteenth century but hoary with tradition. Neither Malmesbury nor Pitt relished the task of having to strip George III of a crown – even a phantom one – in a revolutionary age. It would be wrong to suggest that Malmesbury was to blame for the breakdown of the negotiations in 1796 and 1797 (there were more fundamental reasons for that) but his presence did not signal a "*heureux augure pour la Paix.*"[46]

Whatever may be said about him, Malmesbury was a respected diplomat who had earned his reputation (and his earldom) through talent. Charles, First Marquess Cornwallis came from very different circumstances and had been trained as a professional soldier. He was born in a well established noble family and had inherited the earldom on his father's death in 1762. Upon his return to England in 1793, after a most successful tour as governor-general of India and commander-in-chief in Bengal, he received a marquisate and a seat on the privy council. Earlier, despite his surrender at Yorktown, he had been granted the Garter. Obviously Cornwallis belonged to the upper level of the aristocracy. He had been educated at Eton and Cambridge, served for a time in the House of Commons and took part in 1761 in his first military campaign in Germany. After obtaining a lieutenant-colonelcy he was chosen as aide-de-camp to the King. More promotions followed, in 1770 he was appointed governor of the Tower and his further advancement seemed certain.

Upon the outbreak of war in north America he joined his regiment (which had already crossed the Atlantic) in spite of the fact that he disagreed with the government's policies for the colonies. A firm independence of mind together with a reputation for integrity were the outstanding marks of his character; in parliament he always voted without regard for party. At first he did well enough in the American war. He routed General Gates at Camden and defeated General Greene in 1781. The story of his surrender at Yorktown is too well known to need retelling here; it is of interest however that this debacle was not held against him in Britain. For the next seven years he served in India where he gained distinction as general, administrator and empire builder. Cornwallis captured Bengalore and reduced the lands of Tippoo Sahib by half. His reforms were not yet complete when he returned to England in 1793.

He was now fifty five years old and duly rewarded with honors. The American defeat was ten years behind him, but Cornwallis did not find peace on his return home. The government embroiled in war once more needed his

---

[46] The phrase was used by the French foreign ministry to indicate its displeasure over Malmesbury heading the peace mission in 1797. *Ibid.*, I, p. 156. See also the essay on Malmesbury in Edmund B. D'Auvergne, *Envoys Extraordinary* (London, 1937), pp. 13–88.

services; Cornwallis became master-general of the ordnance with a seat in the cabinet. The struggle with France disturbed him; this was a very different war from fighting raw colonials in the Virginia woods or Indian Sikhs at the Ganges. "It is very difficult to make war, at least upon the Continent, with any prospect of success," he wrote Sir John Shore who had followed him as governor-general in India, "but it is impossible to make peace without fraternizing with the gang of murderers on the other side of the water, and following their bloody example.[47] This strain of pessimism, dating from the period of the Terror, became a constant theme in Cornwallis' letters to his friend and confidant, major general Ross. His defeatism was of the most personal kind.

I confess that I feel an alarm and anxiety about public affairs that entirely destroys the comfort that I hoped to derive from the happy circumstances of my family and fortune.[48]

To Sir John Shore he admitted that since his return his thoughts on public affairs had been "most gloomy." "That we must soon get out of this war is certain. . ."[49]

Since Cornwallis had already known the bitter taste of defeat his fears were more real, while his military expertise could not ignore England's awful circumstances by December 1797.

Torn as we are by faction, without an army, without money, trusting entirely to a navy whom we may not be able to pay, and on whose loyalty, even if we can, no firm reliance is to be placed, how are we to get out of this cursed war without a revolution?[50]

As master-general of the ordnance Cornwallis was also responsible for coastal defense. His efforts to improve Britain's military posture were made more urgent by the expectations of a French invasion.[51] It may have been her good fortune that she never needed to test how well Cornwallis had done his work.

Despite the defeatism of his letters Cornwallis was thought the right man for another important assignment. The cause of parliamentary union with Ireland had failed to gain the necessary converts in Dublin; instead, rebellion and an attempted French invasion had turned the island into a seething

---

[47] *Correspondence of Charles, First Marquis Cornwallis*, ed. by Charles Ross (London, 1859), II, p. 236, Marquis Cornwallis to Sir John Shore, April 17, 1794.

[48] *Ibid.*, II, p. 283, Marquis Cornwallis to Colonel Ross, January 27, 1795.

[49] *Ibid.*, II, p. 295, Cornwallis to Sir John Shore, October 12, 1795.

[50] *Ibid.*, II, p. 328, Cornwallis to Ross, December 15, 1797.

[51] *Ibid.*, II, pp. 283, 311, Cornwallis to Ross, January 27, 1795, November 1, 1796.

cauldron. Cornwallis was appointed lord lieutenant to pacify Ireland and to promote the union with England. Since his tenure of office saw the restoration of order and the approval of the Act of Union he should be praised for his constructive work. Yet a few of his contemporaries denounced him, of whom the Marquis of Buckingham was the most vociferous. The new lord lieutenant dealt mildly with the rebels to regain peace, he paid many political and social bribes (in terms of noble titles) to obtain the votes in favor of the union in the Irish parliament, and he tried to separate the political union from any promises of greater religious liberty for the Irish Catholics. The last step was no doubt dictated by London and the experience of Lord Fitzwilliam in 1795. Although each of these measures had sufficient merit to justify them, Buckingham repeatedly charged Cornwallis with "imbecility" and called him an "idiot."[52] Others complained about Cornwallis' conceding ways in seeking to pass the Act of Union.

Cornwallis himself was most unhappy in Dublin. He had accepted the appointment with his usual sense of duty and service, but he detested the demeaning ways of Irish politics. As he expressed it to Ross: "How I long to kick those whom my public duty obliges me to court!"[53] In fact, he saw little hope in the future for either himself or "this wretched country," and predicted "I am doomed to waste the remainder of my life and sacrifice the little reputation which the too partial opinion of the world has allowed me..."[54] He went on of course, complaining all the while that it was impossible to save Ireland. Cornwallis was still in Dublin when Bonaparte seized power; he welcomed it since "it tends to discredit the plan of putting down established governments..."[55] Still, the war continued after "the unprovoked insolence" of Grenville's letter that rejected Bonaparte's first peace offer. "What is now to become of us," sighed Cornwallis, "...would to God that we had peace almost on any terms, for it is evident that we cannot make war."[56]

It may seem that our sketch of Cornwallis is too somber with gloomy details, but not many figures of this period expressed themselves so explicitly. Moreover, his laments did not appear to inhibit his capacity to succeed: when the Act of Union passed the Irish parliament in August 1800, Cornwallis' work was essentially complete. He was succeeded by Lord Hardwicke and returned to England in July 1801. Although anxious for a rest he was almost

[52] Historical Manuscripts Commission, *The Manuscripts of J. B. Fortescue, Esq., preserved at Dropmore*, vol. IV (London, 1905), pp. 369, 373–375, 393, 423, 440, 462, Marquis Buckingham to Lord Grenville, November 10, 12, 13, 23, December 25, 1798, January 14, February 1, 1799.

[53] *Cornwallis Correspondence*, III, pp. 101, 102, Cornwallis to Ross, May 20, June 8, 1799.

[54] *Ibid.*, III, p. 56, Cornwallis to Ross, January 28, 1799.

[55] *Ibid.*, III, p. 148, Cornwallis to Ross, November 29, 1799.

[56] *Ibid.*, III, pp. 277, 292, Cornwallis to Ross, July 11, September 17, 1800.

immediately recommended to the King as commander of the Eastern District. Bonaparte was creating new invasion scares in England. By mid-September he wrote to Ross that he saw no prospects for peace. "I am myself out of sorts, low-spirited and tired of everything..."[57] Two weeks after writing these lines there was a provisional peace and Cornwallis had been chosen to negotiate a definitive treaty. Why this aging paladin had been selected for so important a task remains uncertain. Was it his high noble status that impressed Addington, his success in Ireland or that as a general he might deal more effectively with Bonaparte?

His appointment was ill-advised in every respect: he lacked diplomatic skills or training, he was a defeatist and in poor health, and Cornwallis remained the honorable but unbending Englishman abroad. His age told against him: he tended to be sleepy, lacking in alertness, and he suffered from gout. Those who appointed him to be the British representative at the Amiens conference seem to have had some doubts too. At least, a colonel Littlehales was attached to Cornwallis' entourage and he reported directly to the prime minister on the proceedings and the work of the mission. There were complaints that Cornwallis' slow way of doing business protracted the discussions; perhaps he was just very careful after some nasty tricks by Joseph Bonaparte. But there can be no doubt that Cornwallis deserved better from his country than this assignment. England might not have fared better at Amiens but she could have done no worse had she chosen a more appropriate negotiator.[58]

In order to complete the triptych of ambassadorial portraits we need to consider Sir Nevile Henderson, British ambassador in Berlin from April 1937 till the outbreak of the second world war. He is the best known of the three and probably the least liked. Henderson was a professional diplomat who had served in Constantinople, Egypt, Paris, Yugoslavia and Argentina before his appointment to Berlin. His family had made its wealth in the late Victorian and Edwardian years but had suffered reverses later. Thus Henderson *père* had once reached and then lost the status of well-off landed gentry. This displacement made its mark on Henderson who henceforth sought to typify what he was not: the debonair aristocrat of means.

Historians have not been kind to Sir Nevile, but it has been easy to ridicule and condemn him. Henderson was a snob of limited intelligence, but he might

---

[57] *Ibid.*, III, p. 382, Cornwallis to Ross, September 17, 1801.

[58] For a discussion of Cornwallis' habits at Amiens, see *The Diaries and Letters of Sir George Jackson*, ed. by Lady Jackson (London, 1872), I, p. 74, March 12, 1802. Sir George was the younger brother of Mr. Francis Jackson, British Minister in Paris at the time of the Amiens conference and himself an attaché in the French capital.

have done better if he had called his memoirs "Failure of a Missionary." Completely convinced of the rightness of his cause – the reconciliation of Britain and Germany – he pursued it to the bitter end. Since Germany had been wronged in 1919, Anglo-German friendship could only be assured by rectifying these historical grievances. Another factor in Henderson's make-up was his horror of communism; he detested the Soviet Union and had worked to prevent an Anglo-Soviet pact in which he had no confidence. If there had to be a treaty with Russia, Henderson told Hitler, he preferred that Germany sign one with the Russians.[59]

Before his appointment to Berlin Henderson had set down his views on Anglo-German relations, German expansion and the role of the Soviet Union.[60] He argued that Anglo-German friendship would have no chance if London blocked German expansion in eastern and southeastern Europe; Sir Nevile also proposed a British guarantee to remain neutral in case of a German-Russian war. In effect Henderson suggested that if France were left untouched Hitler could have a free hand in eastern Europe. The British ambassador believed it necessary to allow such German expansion in order to satisfy her political ego which had never achieved fulfillment in the twentieth century. That this encouragement of aggression would violate the rights of Czechs, Poles or Austrians was of no concern to Sir Nevile. The Foreign Office sharply dissented from these views but did not seek to restrain or remove the ambassador. In case it be thought that Henderson was trying to push Germany into war with Russia, such machiavellianism was not only beyond him but he regarded the Germans far more civilized than the Slavs. A Russian victory moreover (always a possibility) would be an unmitigated disaster.

In this policy context Henderson's conduct was entirely sensible. Before leaving for his post he had had a long interview with Chamberlain and understood his aims with respect to Germany. Sir Nevile almost regarded himself as a personal emissary of the new prime minister and reported as much to him as to the Foreign Office. As long as the appeasement of Germany remained Chamberlain's goal Henderson was the logical man in Berlin. He had the confidence of the prime minister who read his reports. The ambassador's relations with the Foreign Office were less friendly (there was irritation over his close ties with Chamberlain) and the Office resented Henderson's heavy (and not always truthful) hand in policy formulation. So

[59] Margaret George, *The Warped Vision. British Foreign Policy, 1933-1939* (Pittsburgh, 1965), p. 208.
[60] Parts of this document are printed in Laurence Thompson, *The Greatest Treason* (New York, 1968), Appendix, pp. 270-274.

long as friendship with Germany remained the announced intention, the ambassador pretty much went his own way, sure of support and certain that the end justified the means. Since appeasement had its enemies he was sure to have his critics, but his errors were overlooked and he was not recalled. Henderson was wrong of course on many things, not just on appeasement which he had not devised, but on internal conditions in Germany, the infrastructure of nazi politics, Hitler versus the "extremists" and much else. He may have served well as representative of Chamberlain's policies; it is more doubtful that he performed competently as his country's observer and ambassador to an acutely dangerous rival.

Like so many appeasers in the 1930's Henderson admired the strength, the dynamic qualities, of the Nazi movement. Cognizant of capitalism's difficulties and the challenges of communism, the British ambassador went further in his admiration of the Nazi system than was wise, but it would not be correct to call him ideologically subservient. Henderson wanted to please Hitler, and here he differs markedly from Cornwallis who detested revolution yet harbored no great admiration for Bonaparte. Of the three ambassadors, the Earl of Malmesbury remained ideologically the most inflexible, but he did not achieve a peace treaty nor negotiate with an autocrat. Cornwallis had the greater responsibility compared with Henderson while the latter appears as a weak and poorly informed observer. Henderson had been selected because he did not dislike the Germans; while this was important it did not assure that he would report to his government in an objective manner. Perhaps this was so because he knew his own country least of all.

Our attempt at portraiture should include three other figures: Sir John Macpherson, Thomas Jones and Sir Horace Wilson. It is not easy to speak of them in a comparative sense. Each was an advisor of sorts, though Macpherson and possibly Jones were mere busybodies. Macpherson remains a shadowy influence and Wilson a distinctly powerful one whose dimensions remain hidden. Thomas Jones was close to Baldwin but had no entree to Chamberlain. These men did not formulate policy but may at crucial moments have influenced the thinking and decisions of the policy makers. They were especially useful in providing information (some of which was patently erroneous), each felt free to offer his advice and all probably exaggerated the importance of their roles.

Sir John Macpherson was an administrator of the East India Company who through corruption, financial talent and intrigue rose to be governor-general of India by 1785. He was a tall, handsome Scot with courteous manners, but he tended to be erratic and at times verged on the hysterical. Cornwallis, who succeeded him as governor-general, called his rule of India "a system of the dirtiest jobbery."[61] On his return to England he sat in the House of Commons and engaged the East India Company in lengthy litigation to obtain a pension for his services. In 1795 the Austrian government solicited his advice on the administration of its finances. Macpherson was a popular figure in society and counted among his friends the Prince of Wales. It was at the latter's house that he met M. Otto, the French commissioner for the exchange of prisoners.

Whether he had been close to Addington before the Speaker succeeded Pitt is not clear, but Macpherson fairly bombarded the new prime minister with lengthy letters offering advice. The gist of these messages was the overwhelming need for peace, the opportunity for Addington to conclude a treaty with Bonaparte, and the latter's good intentions and confidence in the new prime minister. Macpherson was much exercised about a jacobin revival, including in England, if the negotiations failed. He warned Addington to keep power in his own hands, and spoke of the dangers to Ireland and India if war continued. There is some evidence that Macpherson tried to establish direct contact between Addington and Otto, thus bypassing the Foreign Secretary. Macpherson met Otto several times and reported the Frenchman's views to the prime minister.[62] Whether Macpherson spoke to Addington about avoiding alliances and commercial treaties is uncertain, but Glenbervie believed he was mad, Malmesbury thought him too conceding and Lord Holland described him as strange. In the final analysis we cannot be certain that he accomplished anything other than interject himself in the peace negotiations in an officious manner.

For our account a likeness of Thomas Jones needs only to highlight certain features. Born in Wales, Jones was first intended for the ministry, studied moral philosophy but then entered the civil service. During World War I he became assistant, then deputy secretary to the cabinet, and held this position continuously till 1930. He got along well with Lloyd George, a fellow Welshman, did not work easily with MacDonald but was a close friend and confidant of Baldwin. Jones was an important figure in the government during the 1920's (he mediated labor disputes, attended international conferences) and as his influence increased his circle of acquaintances grew. He knew the right people of the London social circuit and met people easily in conversation with the smooth charm of his native province. In 1930 Jones resigned as deputy secretary of the cabinet to become secretary of the Pilgrim

---

[61] *Cornwallis Correspondence*, I, Cornwallis to Henry Dundas, November 1, 1788.
[62] *The Diaries of Sylvester Douglas, Lord Glenbervie*, ed. by Francis Bickley (London, 1928), I, pp. 300–301.

Trust, a private foundation. His close contacts with Baldwin were unaffected by this change.

Jones' role in appeasement extends only to 1937 when Baldwin retired. In these early years of Nazi rule he strongly favored Anglo-German reconciliation. He was a frequent week-ender at Cliveden, the Astor estate, whose guests were open admirers of Nazi methods for dealing with society's problems. Jones' diary gives us some excellent examples of ideological motivations and fears on the upper class level. Nazi Germany was seen as a bulwark against communism, and war with her would be disastrous for Western civilization. Jones with his close ties to Baldwin became an important conduit for this group to persuade the prime minister to get closer to Germany. One way of doing this would be a meeting between Baldwin and Hitler. Ribbentrop invited Jones to Germany where he met the Nazi leaders, including Hitler. Later he accompanied Lloyd George on another visit to the Führer. But Baldwin remained wary of a conclave with Hitler (he had not forgotten a humiliating conference with Poincaré) and Jones' plans never materialized. After Chamberlain became prime minister Jones moved from center stage; he was not particularly friendly with the man from Birmingham whose business friends were very different from Baldwin and his literary interests.

If Jones played no part at the summit of appeasement, the way to Munich had been paved long before Chamberlain. To that effort Jones had contributed his share, and if he had been stopped short in the appeasement of Germany he owed this more to Baldwin than his own wisdom. His later denunciation of Munich which "filled [him] with gloom and shame" for the abject surrender it implied, does not make sense.[63] Had he forgotten his response to the Rhineland crisis, the Spanish civil war or the warnings of Colonel Lindbergh? One suspects that his inability to participate in the decisions affected his attitude. Had Jones been a member of the Chamberlain team, and been at Munich, he might have sung its praise and commended its achievement.

Unlike Jones, Sir Horace Wilson, chief industrial adviser to the government and posted for service with the prime minister since 1935, was clearly at the center of events. Any attempt to portray him must be tentative. His death in 1971 had not been preceded by the usual published account of his role. Yet for three years, from 1937 till the fall of Chamberlain in 1940, he was the single most powerful adviser of the prime minister. The outline of his career is well known: he had risen in the civil service as an experienced labor mediator.

---

[63] Jones, *Diary*, p. 409.

MacDonald had promoted him to chief industrial adviser for the government and Baldwin had invented the position "for service with the Prime Minister." But Wilson truly came into his own with Chamberlain who greatly valued his advice and capacity for succinctness.[64]

As far as can be determined, Sir Horace had no experience in foreign affairs and spoke no foreign languages. His talents were administrative: he could quickly summarize a situation or document, he had the gift of precise expression and he was experienced in conciliation. In the latter role he had developed the habit of minimizing differences and stressing what both sides held in common. Wilson completely supported Chamberlain's efforts for the appeasement of Germany and was regarded as pro-German by the Nazis themselves.[65] The flexibility of his mind had given Wilson a talent for devising face-saving formulas rather than clear-cut policies. Since Chamberlain pursued appeasement in spite of evidence and advice to the contrary, Sir Horace reinforced the prime minister's worst tendencies. As one critic put it: "his influence was almost wholly bad . . ."[66] But he was a tireless worker, self-effacing, soft spoken and yet immensely powerful whose only concern seemed to be his job, keeping his influence and serving his chief.

This "ideal" civil servant accompanied Chamberlain on his three trips to Germany, visited Hitler in between, and negotiated with German diplomats without Foreign Office interference. Wilson had an office at 10 Downing Street and saw the prime minister virtually every day. His role in the abortive economic discussions with Germany, which took place on the eve of World War II, was crucial in the continuation of a "hidden appeasement" despite the occupation of Prague. And yet we do not know a great deal about the man, his motives and the nature of his relationship with Chamberlain. Was he the prime minister's idea man or trouble shooter, a source of inspiration or only a reliable assistant? Why was Wilson pro-German? Did he fear German power, or was he only trying to prove his loyalty to his master's policies? Did this unassuming civil servant know ideological fears, or was he engaged in a careful game of playing for time.[67] Regardless of the answers, his influence went well beyond that of Thomas Jones and certainly surpassed the role of Sir John Macpherson. Yet the complete history of Sir Horace Wilson remains to be written.

[64] Feiling, op. cit., p. 327.

[65] Martin Gilbert and Richard Gott, The Appeasers (Boston, 1963), p. 79. See also the summary and evaluation of Sir Horace Wilson's character, pp. 376–377.

[66] Ibid., p. 377.

[67] Wilson was in fact concerned about communism. See Thorne, op. cit., p. 15; Keith Robbins, Munich, 1938 (London, 1968), pp. 241, 301–302. For the Chamberlain-Wilson relationship, Gilbert and Gott, op. cit., pp. 55–57.

There are obvious differences as well as similarities in our descriptions of Britain's leading figures and minor functionaries. In each epoch the British nation was at bay. Faced with a superior foe her leaders groped for a response. Pitt fought and negotiated, Baldwin temporized, Addington and Chamberlain resorted to appeasement and their foreign secretaries followed suit. Ambassadors and advisers acted generally in accordance with the government's policies. The pursuit of peace was a necessity at such times and appeasement the experiment that seemed worth the chance. If it failed it would not be because Britons had refused to try it.

CHAPTER VI

THE BALANCE SHEET

It is easy to forget the basic purpose of appeasement. In the search for motive or the analysis of comparable events the fundamental issue can be overlooked. Appeasement sought to preserve peace or to establish it, and unless one believes that peace is not worthwhile, then that objective is a noble one. Peace may be invoked to justify ill-advised policies (to reduce defense expenditures) or put to an unworthy use (to maintain a particular social structure). Even when peace is obtained at an unreasonable cost, the price does not detract from its inherent value. This strong moral quality gave appeasement the conviction that was so difficult to resist.

Earlier we made a point that needs repeating here. To a certain extent appeasement was an accepted practice in diplomacy insofar as the give and take of negotiations led to concessions by one side or the other for the sake of agreement. It may be deceptive to use the term appeasement for this process now, inasmuch as the term has come to mean a one-sided surrender. In conventional diplomacy both sides engage in quid pro quos, although in practice one party might pay the lion's share for an accord. Nevertheless, the expectation of the English travelers to Amiens and Munich was that, though substantial appeasement on their part might be necessary, not all the concessions would come from one side. In terms of traditional diplomacy this attitude was reasonable, and major concessions, though not pleasant, could be made in return for stable agreements. When this "traditional" appeasement failed because it went far beyond the reasonable limits, the term quickly became an odious one.[1]

But, it may be argued, the practitioners of "traditional" appeasement had been warned that major concessions would not work. The career of Bonaparte and the record of Hitler were replete with treachery; they would not submit to conventional behavior in diplomatic terms. In the search for peace

---

[1] This is the point made by Martin Gilbert in *The Roots of Appeasement* (New York, 1966), pp. 179, 186.

this advice was generally ignored and instead Addington and Chamberlain went to great length to express their good will, even their friendship for the regimes in Paris and Berlin. Some of this rhetoric may be discounted as gestures which cost little, but the avowedly friendly feelings and efforts to establish closer relations may have encouraged the First Consul and the Führer to act more aggressively. The ill will shown revolutionary France and Weimar Germany led later prime ministers to reverse British policies so drastically that it went beyond "traditional" appeasement even before Amiens and Munich. Were they justified in following in a revolutionary age a foreign policy that went contrary to the advice they received? Obviously their quest for peace figures strongly in this consideration, but our conclusion must be a negative one.

It should be explained that in denying the justification for appeasing Bonaparte or Hitler the slim chance of success is uppermost in our mind. But leaving this efficiency factor aside for a moment, were there moral justifications for appeasement? With peace as its aim one could easily say yes; so too perhaps one could argue in its favor to correct previous wrongs. On these moral grounds one could theoretically be in favor of appeasement. Theoretical morality has an odd way of going astray in practice, however. No moral arguments to appease one country should ever be invoked if it involves the sacrifice of another land. What sort of peace would it be anyway if to obtain agreement to keep quiet on the part of one people would require strangling another? And if the survival of Western civilization depended on the extinction of Czechoslovakia, how long would it be before this Moloch would demand another sacrifice? These are not the arguments of cautious leaders striving for peace but the anxious pleas of weary men.[2]

Once the Amiens treaty and the Munich pact had been signed it was no longer a question whether it should be concluded or if it was moral but how long it would work. Was appeasement an effective policy for providing peace? The historical record is not encouraging. In 1801 Great Britain had no prospects of defeating Bonaparte and, despite her victories in Egypt and at Copenhagen, desired only to end the war. The appeasement of Bonaparte cost her nearly all the colonies she had conquered in nine years of fighting. She gained the breathing space, the time to recover, but it was of short duration. All the while Bonaparte continued to extend his power on the continent; Italy, Switzerland and the Low Countries were controlled or occupied by French troops. It was no small concern to London that this violated the treaty

---

[2] The moral contradictions of appeasement are discussed by Laurence Lafore, *The End of Glory* (Philadelphia, 1970), pp. 232–233.

of Lunéville. Could the British government permit itself to relax and accept the benefits of peace under these circumstances?

While the English people enjoyed a rest Addington cut taxes and reduced the military establishment. But within a year of signing the treaty of Amiens he had to reverse his policies and prepare once more for war. It is true that Britain benefitted from the pause that the peace conferred; even Windham later confessed he had been wrong in opposing the Amiens agreement. Yet the period of peace was so short, at most a year, that one must seriously question if Addington's appeasement accomplished its purpose. As a peace policy sustained at very great expense its duration was too limited to be effective.

The relaxation of tension was even shorter after the Munich agreement. Well before the occupation of Prague Hitler had informed the Polish government of his wishes about the Corridor and Danzig. Chamberlain's expectations of his appeasement policies after Munich are far less clear. On the one hand the prime minister spoke of "peace for our time," and he grumbled in late October that "a lot of people . . . seem to me to be losing their heads, and talking and thinking as though Munich had made war more, instead of less, imminent."[3] But he knew that he had negotiated out of weakness. He told the King in the middle of October that ". . . future policy must be the cultivation of friendly relations combined with intensified rearmament. One must be strong in order to negotiate. . ."[4] And yet while the acceleration of existing rearmament programs was ordered, new expenditures were not. The prime minister rejected the thought that his agreement with Hitler would mean an expanded rearmament program, only a quicker completion of existing ones. By December he confided to his cabinet that ". . . Hitler's next move, which would be eastwards, in which case we might well not be involved at all."[5]

Whatever his expectations were, and Chamberlain may not have been certain in his own mind what the future held, the outcome of appeasement was not peace so much as a period of watchful waiting. As an effective peace policy, then, appeasement never held much promise after the Munich pact. The gradual destruction of Czechoslovakia created more rather than less tension in central Europe. Can one, however, argue from a different standpoint that appeasement was effective because it gave Britain the additional time to prepare for war? Had Chamberlain's appeasement policies been the essential prerequisite for the Battle of Britain? This point has been the subject of much debate, but whatever its validity (remembering that in 1938 Germany

---

[3] Keith Feiling, *The Life of Neville Chamberlain* (London, 1946), p. 386.
[4] As quoted in Keith Robbins, *Munich, 1938* (London, 1968), p. 330.
[5] Keith Middlemas, *Diplomacy of Illusion: The British Government and Germany, 1937–39* (London, 1972), pp. 421, 427.

too was less prepared for war than in 1939) it was not what Chamberlain had intended. He always believed that the Munich agreement was right for its own sake, as the apogee of appeasement, rather than an instrument by which Britain gained valuable time. Chamberlain rejected the inevitability of war and the appeasement of Germany was to prevent conflict rather than delay it.

Although appeasement was a distinct failure as an effective policy for preserving peace, it accomplished something quite different: the realization by the British people of the necessity for war if it wished to preserve England's freedom. In the wake of the Amiens treaty and the Munich pact with its disappointments, frustration and disputes it became clear that coexistence with Bonaparte or Hitler was impossible. Europe would know no peace until England or its continental enemy had been overcome. The acceptance of this hard fact was slow in coming, but its progress was outlined by Henry Addington on the eve of the great struggle with Napoleon. As he explained it to the Earl of Malmesbury in February, 1803:

His maxim ... from the moment he took office was, first to make peace, and then to preserve it, under certain reservations in his own mind, if France chose, and as long as France chose ... till such time as France (as he ever foresaw it must happen) had filled the measure of her folly, and had put herself completely in the wrong, not only by repeated and intolerable acts of unprovoked insolence and presumption ... That simple acts of insolence and impertinence, however grating, he had passed over, because he never would put on a par the sober and antient dignity of Great Britain with the infatuated mushroom arrogance of Buonaparte ... he [Addington] *had waited till insolence was coupled with hostility*, or (which was the same) hostile declarations, before he moved.[6]

Addington felt certain in his own mind that

... he was not of that species of Minister who, to preserve peace, would tamely submit to any ignominy or disgrace, and to let the country be trampled on with impunity! That he certainly, in common with all men in their senses, preferred a state of peace to one of war; but when he was *in the right*, and felt himself so completely in *the right* as on the present occasion, he was, not as an *event*, but as a *measure* of responsibility, perfectly indifferent whether it was to be peace or war...[7]

How could Bonaparte or Hitler appreciate that England's patience had run its course, or that the "experimental peace" could not survive the test of coexistence? But appeasement had always been a dubious policy, involving many risks and without the assurance of solid returns. Why then, had

---

[6] *Diaries and Correspondence of James Harris, First Earl of Malmesbury*, ed. by his grandson, the third Earl (London, 1845), IV, pp. 213-214, February 19, 1803. The italics appear in the text.
[7] *Ibid.*, IV, p. 215, February 19, 1803. The italics appear in the text.

Addington or Chamberlain undertaken it? The simplest answer lies in England's circumstances in 1801 and 1938. Her leaders were bound to try it because their options were very limited. Neither resources nor motivations at that moment favored an aggressive policy, although within a relatively short time Great Britain once more found herself and reverted to asserting her influence. Perhaps the brief interlude of peace gave her the opportunity to see her situation in a more realistic light. Almost too late she abandoned concessions and decided to challenge the pretensions of her continental enemies. "The Englishman's truly distinctive disease is his cherished habit of waiting until the 13th hour."[8] Once that hour struck, however, appeasement ceased to be a policy.

---

[8] Arnold Toynbee, quoted in *Time*, August 4, 1975, p. 30.

BIBLIOGRAPHY

I. DOCUMENTS

a) unpublished

"Addington papers," Public Record Office, Exeter, Devonshire.

"Chatham papers," Public Record Office, London, PRO 30/8, 2nd series.

"Liverpool papers," Manuscript Room, British Museum, Add. mss. 38237, 38238, 38312, 38316, 38318.

"Windham papers," Manuscript Room, British Museum, Add. mss. 37844, 37846, 37847, 37922.

b) published

Authentic Copies of the Papers relative to the Commencement of Negotiations for Peace with France. London, 1800.

Authentic Official Documents relative to the Negotiation with France. London, 1803.

Celebrated Speeches of Chatham, Burke, and Erskine. Philadelphia, 1840.

English Historical Documents, vol. XI, 1783–1832, ed. by A. Aspinall and E. Anthony Smith. London, 1959.

Fox, Charles James. *Speeches during the French Revolution.* London, 1924.

Historical Manuscripts Commission. *Manuscripts of Earl Bathurst preserved at Cirencester Park.* London, 1923.

—. *The Manuscripts of J. B. Fortescue, Esq., preserved at Dropmore*, vols. II–VII. London, 1894–1910.

Official Papers, relative to the Preliminaries of London and the Treaty of Amiens. 2nd ed. London, 1803.

The Paget Papers. London, 1896. 2 vols.

The Parliamentary History of England from the Earliest Period to the Year 1803. vol. 36. London, 1820.

The Political Memoranda of Francis, Fifth Duke of Leeds. ed. by Oscar Browning. Royal Historical Society, 1884.

Select Speeches of the Rt. Honourable William Windham, ed. by Robert Walsh. Philadelphia, 1837.

A Selection from the Speeches of the late Lord King, ed. by Earl Fortescue. London, 1844.

The Speeches of the Right Hon. Lord Erskine at the Bar and in Parliament. London, 1847. 4 vols.

The Speeches of the Right Honourable George Canning, ed. by R. Therry. London, 1830. 6 vols.

The Speeches of the Right Honourable Charles James Fox in the House of Commons. London, 1815. 6 vols.

The Speeches of the Right Honourable Richard Brinsley Sheridan. London, 1842. 3 vols.

The Substance of the Speech of the Right Honourable Henry Addington in the Committee of Ways and Means, December 10, 1802. London, 1803.

The War Speeches of William Pitt the Younger, selected by R. Coupland. 3rd. ed. Oxford, 1940.

WHITWORTH, CHARLES. *England and Napoleon in 1803, being the despatches of Lord Whitworth and others*, ed. by Oscar Browning. London, 1887.

The Windham Papers, with an introduction by the Rt. Hon. The Earl of Rosebery. Boston, 1913. 2 vols.

WYVILL, CHRISTOPHER. *Political Papers*. York, 1794–1802. 4 vols.

2. BIOGRAPHIES, DIARIES, LETTERS, MEMOIRS

ALISON, SIR ARCHIBALD. *Lives of Lord Castlereagh and Sir Charles Stewart*. Edinburgh, 1861. 3 vols.

AUCKLAND: *The Journal and Correspondence of William, Lord Auckland*. London, 1862. 4 vols.

The Autobiography of Arthur Young, ed. by M. Betham-Edwards. London, 1898.

AVON: *The Memoirs of Anthony Eden, Earl of Avon*, vol. I "Facing the Dictators." Boston, 1962.

BAINES, E. *The Life of Edward Baines*. London, 1851.

Barnard Letters, 1778–1824, ed. by Anthony Powell. London, 1928.

BARTLETT, C. J. *Castlereagh*. New York, 1966.

BENTHAM: *The Works of Jeremy Bentham.* Edinburgh, 1843. 11 vols.

BERESFORD: *The Correspondence of the Right Hon. John Beresford,* ed. by William Beresford. London, 1854. 2 vols.

BIRKENHEAD, THE EARL OF. *Halifax, The Life of Lord Halifax.* London, 1965.

BOURRIENNE, LOUIS ANTOINE FAUVELET DE. *Memoirs of Napoleon Bonaparte.* New York, 1885. 4 vols.

Brief Memoirs of the Right Honourable Henry Addington's Administration. London, 1802.

BRINTON, CRANE. *The Lives of Talleyrand.* New York, 1963.

Brougham and his early Friends: Letters of James Loch, 1798–1809. London, 1908. 3 vols.

BUCKINGHAM AND CHANDOS, DUKE OF. *Memoirs of the Court and Cabinets of George the Third.* London, 1853–1855. 4 vols.

BURKE: *The Works of the Right Honourable Edmund Burke.* London, 1899. 12 vols.

BURNEY, FRANCES, MADAME D'ARBLAY. *Diary and Letters.* London, 1905. 6 vols.

CAMPBELL, LORD JOHN. *The Lives of the Lord Chancellors and Keepers of the Great Seal of England.* Philadelphia, 1851. 7 vols.

CASTLEREAGH: *Memoirs and Correspondence, and other Papers of Viscount Castlereagh,* ed. by his brother, Marquess of Londonderry. London, 1848–1853. 12 vols.

CHATTERTON, E. KEBLE. *England's Greatest Statesman: A Life of William Pitt, 1759–1806.* Indianapolis, 1930.

COBBETT, WILLIAM. *Letters to the Right Honourable Lord Hawkesbury and to the Right Honourable Henry Addington on the Peace with Buonaparte.* London, 1802. 2nd ed.

—. *The Life and Letters of William Cobbett in England and America.* London, 1913. 2 vols.

COLCHESTER: *The Diary and Correspondence of Charles Abbot, Lord Colchester,* ed. by his son Charles, Lord Colchester. London, 1861. 3 vols.

COLE, G. D. H. *The Life of William Cobbett.* London, 1924.

COLERIDGE, SAMUEL TAYLOR. *Essays on his own Times.* London, 1850. 3 vols.

—. *Unpublished Letters of Samuel Taylor Coleridge,* ed. by Earl Leslie Griggs. New Haven, 1933. 2 vols.

COLVILLE, J. R. *Man of Valour. The Life of Field-Marshal The Viscount Gort.* London, 1972.

CORNWALLIS: *Correspondence of Charles, First Marquis Cornwallis,* ed. with notes by Charles Ross, Esq. London, 1859. 3 vols.

COSTIGAN, GIOVANNI. *Sir Robert Wilson: A soldier of fortune in the Napoleonic Wars.* Madison, 1932.

DERRY, JOHN W. *William Pitt.* New York, 1963.

DRINKWATER, JOHN. *Charles James Fox.* London, 1928.

DUNFERMLINE, JAMES LORD. *Lieutenant-General Sir Ralph Abercromby K.B.* Edinburgh, 1861.

ELDON: *The Public and Private Life of Lord Chancellor Eldon, with selections from his correspondence.* London, 1844. 3 vols.

EHRMAN, JOHN. *The Younger Pitt. The Years of Acclaim.* New York, 1969.

FARINGTON: *The Farington Diary*, ed. by James Greig. New York, 1923–1926. 8 vols.

FEILING, KEITH. *The Life of Neville Chamberlain.* London, 1946.

FITZMAURICE, LORD. *Life of William, Earl of Shelburne, first Marquess of Lansdowne.* London, 1912. 2 vols. 2nd ed.

FOSTER, VERE. *The Two Duchesses.* London, 1898.

FOX: *Memorials and Correspondence of Charles James Fox*, ed. by Lord John Russell. London, 1854. 4 vols.

The Francis Letters, ed. by Beata Francis, New York, n.d. 2 vols.

FRANCIS: *Memoirs of Sir Philip Francis*, ed. by Joseph Parkes and Herman Merivale. London, 1867. 2 vols.

FURBER, HOLDEN. *Henry Dundas, First Viscount Melville, 1742–1811.* London, 1931.

GEORGE III: *The later Correspondence of George III*, ed. by A. Aspinall. Cambridge, 1963–1968. Vols. II, III, IV.

—. *The Letters of King George III*, ed. by Bonamy Dobree. London, 1935.

GEORGE, PRINCE OF WALES: *The Correspondence of George, Prince of Wales, 1770–1812*, ed. by A. Aspinall. London, 1965–1967. Vols. III, IV.

Georgiana. Extracts from the Correspondence of Georgiana, Duchess of Devonshire, ed. by the Earl of Bessborough. London, 1955.

GIBSON, EDWARD, LORD ASHBOURNE. *Pitt: Some Chapters of his Life and Times.* London, 1898.

GIFFORD, JOHN. *A History of the Political Life of the Right Honourable William Pitt.* London, 1809. 6 vols.

GLENBERVIE: *The Diaries of Sylvester Douglas, Lord Glenbervie*, ed. by Francis Bickley. London, 1928. 2 vols.

GOWER, LORD GRANVILLE LEVESON. *Private Correspondence, 1781–1821.* London, 1917. 2 vols.

GRAY, DENIS. *Spencer Perceval*. Manchester, 1963.

GREY, LT. GENERAL, THE HON. C. *Some Account of the Life and Opinions of Charles, Second Earl Grey*. London, 1861.

HAMMOND, J. L. LE. B. *Charles James Fox*. London, 1903.

HENDERSON, SIR NEVILE. *Failure of a Mission*. New York, 1940.

HOBHOUSE, CHRISTOPHER. *Fox*. London, 1934.

HOLLAND: *The Journal of Elizabeth Lady Holland (1791–1811)*, ed. by the Earl of Ilchester. New York, 1908. 2 vols.

HOLLAND, HENRY RICHARD, LORD. *Memoirs of the Whig Party during my time*. London, 1852–1854. 2 vols.

Intimate Society Letters of the Eighteenth Century, ed. by the Duke of Argyll. New York, 1910. 2 vols.

JACKSON: *The Diaries and Letters of Sir George Jackson*, ed. by Lady Jackson. London, 1872. 2 vols.

JONES, M. G. *Hannah More*. Cambridge, 1952.

JONES, THOMAS. *A Diary with Letters, 1931–1950*. London, 1954.

The Journal of Mary Frampton, 1779–1846, ed. by H. G. Mundy. London, 1885.

KING: *The Life and Correspondence of Rufus King*, ed. by Charles R, King. New York, 1894–1900. 6 vols.

LASCELLES, EDWARD. *The Life of Charles James Fox*. London, 1936.

LEIGH, IONE. *Castlereagh*. London, 1951.

LENNOX: *The Life and Letters of Lady Sarah Lennox, 1745–1826*, ed. by the Countess of Ilchester. London, 1901–1902. 2 vols.

MACKINTOSH: *Memoirs of the Life of the Right Honourable Sir James Mackintosh*, ed. by his son, Robert J. Mackintosh. Boston, 1853. 2 vols.

—. *The Miscellaneous Works of Sir James Mackintosh*. Philadelphia, 1853.

MACLEOD, IAIN. *Neville Chamberlain*. New York, 1962.

MALMESBURY: *Diaries and Correspondence of James Harris, First Earl of Malmesbury*, ed. by the 3rd Earl. London, 1845. 4 vols.

—. *A Series of Letters of the First Earl of Malmesbury, 1745–1820*, ed. by the Rt. Hon. Earl of Malmesbury. London, 1870. 2 vols.

MANN, GOLO. *Secretary of Europe. The Life of Friedrich Gentz*. New Haven, 1946.

MARKHAM, FELIX. *Napoleon*. New York, 1963.

MARRIOTT, J. A. R. *George Canning and his time: a political study*. London, 1903.

MARTIN, THEODORE. *A Life of Lord Lyndhurst*. London, 1883.

MATHESON, CYRIL. *The Life of Henry Dundas, First Viscount Melville, 1742–1811*. London, 1933.

Memoirs of the Public Life and Administration of the Right Honourable the Earl of Liverpool. London, 1827.

MIDDLEMAS, KEITH AND JOHN BARNES. *Baldwin. A Biography*. New York, 1970.

MILES: *The Correspondence of William Augustus Miles on the French Revolution, 1789–1817*, ed. by the Reverend C. P. Miles. London, 1890. 2 vols.

MINTO: *Life and Letters of Sir Gilbert Elliot, First Earl of Minto*, ed. by the Countess of Minto. London, 1874. 3 vols.

MOORE, THOMAS. *Memoirs of the Life of the Right Honourable Richard Brinsley Sheridan*. London, 1825. 2 vols.

NICOLSON, HAROLD. *Diaries and Letters, 1930–1939*. Vol. I. New York, 1966.

OLPHIN, H. K. *George Tierney*. London, 1934.

OLSON, ALISON G. *The Radical Duke. Career and Correspondence of Charles Lennox, third Duke of Richmond*. Oxford, 1961.

The Paget Brothers, 1790–1840, ed. by Lord Hylton. London, 1918.

PATTERSON, M. W. *Sir Frances Burdett and His Times (1770–1844)*. London, 1931. 2 vols.

PELLEW, GEORGE. *The Life and Correspondence of the Right Honble. Henry Addington, First Viscount Sidmouth*. London, 1847. 3 vols.

A later Pepys. The Correspondence of Sir William Weller Pepys, ed. by Alice C. C. Gaussen. London, 1904. 2 vols.

PETRIE, SIR CHARLES. *George Canning*. London, 1930.

—. *Lord Liverpool and his times*. London, 1954.

PHIPPS, EDMUND. *Memoirs of the Political and Literary Life of Robert Plumer Ward*. London, 1850. 2 vols.

PRETYMAN, GEORGE, BISHOP TOMLINE. *Life of Pitt*. Vol. I–III. London, 1821. Vol. IV. London, 1903.

ROBINSON, HENRY CRABB. *Diary, Reminiscences and Correspondence*. Boston, 1871. 2 vols.

ROLO, P. J. V. *George Canning: Three Biographical Studies*. London, 1965.

ROSE: *The Diaries and Correspondence of the Right Hon. George Rose*, ed. by the Rev. Leveson Vernon-Harcourt. London, 1860. 2 vols.

ROSE, J. HOLLAND. *William Pitt and the Great War*. London, 1911.

ROSEBERY, LORD. *Pitt*. London, 1891.

RUDKIN, OLIVE D. *Thomas Spence and his connections*. New York, 1927.

RUSSELL, EARL. *The Life and Times of Charles James Fox*. London, 1859–1866. 3 vols.

SALISBURY, MARQUESS OF. *Essays*. London, 1905. 2 vols.

SANDFORD, MRS. HENRY. *Thomas Poole and his friends*. London, 1888. 2 vols.

SETON-KARR, W. S. *The Marquess Cornwallis*. Oxford, 1890.

SHERIDAN: *The Letters of Richard Brinsley Sheridan*, ed. by Cecil Price. Oxford, 1966. 3 vols.

SOUTHEY, ROBERT. *Letters from England*, ed. by Jack Simmons. London, 1951.

—. *New Letters of Robert Southey*, ed. by Kenneth Curry. New York, 1965.

SPENCER: *Private Papers of George, second Earl Spencer. First Lord of the Admiralty, 1794–1801*. Navy Records Society, 1913–1924. 4 vols.

STANHOPE, EARL. *Life of the Right Honourable William Pitt*. London, 1861–1862. 4 vols.

STANHOPE, PHILIP HENRY, FIFTH EARL. *Notes of Conversations with the Duke of Wellington, 1831–1851*. London, 1888.

STAPLETON, AUGUSTUS GRANVILLE. *George Canning and his times*. London, 1859.

ST. VINCENT: *Letters of Admiral of the Fleet, the Earl of St. Vincent*, ed. by David B. Smith. London, 1922–1927. 2 vols.

TEIGNMOUTH: *Memoir of the Life and Correspondence of John Lord Teignmouth*. London, 1843. 2 vols.

TREVELYAN, GEORGE M. *Lord Grey of the Reform Bill*. New York, 1920.

WAKEMAN, HENRY O. *Life of Charles James Fox*. London, 1890.

WARNER, OLIVER. *Victory: the life of Lord Nelson*. Boston, 1958.

The Wellesley Papers. The Life and Correspondence of Richard Marquess Wellesley. London, 1914. 2 vols.

WICKHAM: *The Correspondence of the Right Honourable William Wickham*, ed. by William Wickham. London, 1870. 2 vols.

WILBERFORCE: *The Correspondence of William Wilberforce*, ed. by his sons R. I. and S. Wilberforce. London, 1840. 2 vols.

The Life of William Wilberforce. London, 1838. 5 vols.

Private Papers of William Wilberforce, ed. by A. M. Wilberforce. London, 1897.

WILLIAMS, ORLO. *Lamb's Friend the Census-Taker: Life and Letters of John Rickman*. Boston, 1912.

WILLSON, BECKLES. *George III.* London, 1907.

WILSON, P. W. *William Pitt the Younger.* New York, 1930.

WINDHAM: *The Diary of the Right Honourable William Windham, 1784–1810,* ed. by Mrs. Henry Baring. London, 1866.

WOODFORDE, JAMES. *The diary of a country parson, 1758–1802.* London, 1949. World Classics ed.

WORTLEY, E. STUART. *A Prime Minister and His Son: From the Correspondence of the 3rd Earl of Bute and of Lt.-General The Hon. Charles Stuart.* London, 1925.

WRENCH, JOHN EVELYN. *Geoffrey Dawson and Our Times.* London, 1955.

The Wynne Diaries, ed. by Anne Fremantle, Vol. III 1798–1820. London, 1940.

YONGE, CHARLES D. *The Life and Administration of Robert Banks, Second Earl of Liverpool.* London, 1868. 3 vols.

YOUNG, G. M. *Stanley Baldwin.* London, 1952.

ZIEGLER, PHILIP. *Addington. A Life of Henry Addington, First Viscount Sidmouth.* New York, 1965.

3. SPECIALIZED STUDIES

ADAMS, E. D. *The Influence of Grenville on Pitt's Foreign Policy, 1787–1798.* Washington, 1904.

ADAMS, W. H. D. *English Party Leaders and English Parties.* London, 1878. 2 vols.

ALGER, J. G. *Napoleon's British Visitors and Captives, 1801–1815.* Westminster, 1904.

Annals of Great Britain (1760–1801). Edinburgh, 1807. 3 vols.

Appeasement. A novel by George A. Birmingham. London, 1939.

ASHTON, JOHN. *The Dawn of the XIXth Century in England.* New York, 1886.

ASPINALL, A. *The Early English Trade Unions.* London, 1949.

ASPINALL, A. *Politics and the Press, c. 1780–1850.* London, 1949.

BAGOT, JOSCELINE. *George Canning and his friends.* London, 1909. 2 vols.

BARNES, DONALD G. *George III and William Pitt, 1783–1806.* Stanford, 1939.

BIRLEY, ROBERT. *The English Jacobins, from 1789 to 1802.* London, 1924.

BISSET, ROBERT. *The History of the Reign of George III to the termination of the late war.* London, 1803. 6 vols.

BORAN, MOTHER FRANCIS DE SALES. *The British Peace Attempts of 1795–1797.* Unpublished Ph.D. dissertation, Fordham University, 1958.

BOWLES, JOHN. *Reflections at the Conclusions of the War*. London, 1801.

BOWMAN, HERVEY M. *Preliminary Stages of the Peace of Amiens*. Toronto, 1899.

BRAILSFORD, H. N. *Shelley, Godwin and Their Circle*. New York, 1951. 2nd ed.

BRANDT, OTTO. *England und die Napoleonische Weltpolitik, 1800–1803*. Heidelberg, 1916. 2nd ed.

BRIGGS, ASA. *The Age of Improvement*. London, 1959.

BRINTON, CRANE. *A Decade of Revolution, 1789–1799*. New York, 1934.

BROCK, W. R. *Lord Liverpool and Liberal Toryism, 1820 to 1827*. Cambridge, 1941.

BRODERICK, GEORGE C. AND J. K. FOTHERINGHAM. *The History of England; From Addington's Administration to the close of William IV's reign (1801–1837)*. London, 1906.

BROWN, PHILIP ANTHONY. *The French Revolution in English History*. New York, 1924.

BROWNE, G. LATHOM. *Narratives of State Trials in the Nineteenth Century*. London, 1882. 2 vols.

BRUUN, GEOFFREY. *Europe and the French Imperium, 1799–1814*. New York, 1963.

BRYANT, ARTHUR. *The Years of Endurance, 1793–1802*. London, 1942.

—. *Years of Victory, 1802–1812*. New York, 1945.

The Cambridge Modern History. Vols. VIII, IX. Cambridge, 1907, 1909.

CARSWELL, JOHN. *The Old Cause: Three biographical studies in Whiggism*. London, 1954.

CHURCHILL, WINSTON S. *The Gathering Storm*. Boston, 1948.

CLIFFORD, JAMES L., ed. *Man versus Society in Eighteenth Century Britain*. Cambridge, 1968.

COBBETT, WILLIAM. *A collection of facts and observations relative to the peace with Bonaparte*. London, 1801.

COLVIN, IAN. *The Chamberlain Cabinet*. New York, 1971.

CONE, CARL B. *Burke and the Nature of Politics*. Lexington, 1964. 2 vols.

—. *The English Jacobins. Reformers in late 18th century England*. New York, 1968.

COWIE, L. W. *British History, 1763–1914*. London, 1966.

D'AUVERGNE, EDMUND B. *Envoys Extraordinary*. London, 1937.

DAVIS, H. W. CARLESS. *The Age of Grey and Peel*. Oxford, 1929.

DECHAMPS, JULES. *Les Iles Britanniques et la Révolution Française (1789–1803)*. Brussels, 1949.

DEUTSCH, HAROLD C. *The Genesis of Napoleonic Imperialism*. Cambridge, Mass., 1938.

The Diplomats, 1919–1939, ed. by Gordon A. Craig and Felix Gilbert. New York, 1963. 2 vols.

EBBINGHAUS, THERESE. *Napoleon, England und die Presse (1800–1803)*. Munich, 1914.

EINZIG, PAUL. *Appeasement, before, during and after the war*. London, 1942.

ERDMAN, DAVID V. *Blake: Prophet against Empire*. Princeton, 1954.

EUBANK, KEITH. *Munich*. Norman, 1963.

EYCK, ERICH. *Pitt versus Fox: Father and Son, 1735–1806*. London, 1950.

FEILING, KEITH. *The Second Tory Party, 1714–1832*. London, 1938.

FESTING, GABRIELLE. *John Hookman Frere and his Friends*. London, 1899.

A few Cursory Remarks upon the State of Parties, during the Administration of the Right Honourable Henry Addington. By a Near Observer. London, 1803.

FITZPATRICK, W. J. *Secret Service under Pitt*. London, 1892.

FOORD, ARCHIBALD S. *His Majesty's Opposition, 1714–1830*. Oxford, 1964.

FORTESCUE, J. W. *British Statesmen of the Great War, 1793–1814*. Oxford, 1911.

FREMANTLE, ALAN S. *England in the nineteenth century, 1801–1805*. London, 1929.

FRISCHAUER, PAUL. *England's Years of Danger*. New York, 1938.

GANNON, FRANKLIN REID. *The British Press and Germany, 1936–1939*. Oxford, 1971.

GEORGE, MARGARET. *The Warped Vision: British Foreign Policy, 1933–1939*. Pittsburgh, 1965.

GILBERT, MARTIN. *Britain and Germany between the Wars*. New York, 1967.

—. *The Roots of Appeasement*. New York, 1966.

GILBERT, MARTIN AND RICHARD GOTT. *The Appeasers*. Boston, 1963.

GILL, CONRAD. *The Naval Mutinies of 1797*. Manchester, 1913.

GOTTSCHALK, LOUIS R. *The Era of the French Revolution*. Boston, 1929.

GRAINGER, J. H. *Character and Style in English Politics*. Cambridge, 1969.

GRAVES, ROBERT AND ALAN HODGE. *The Long Week-End*. New York, 1963.

HALÉVY, ELIE. *A History of the English People in the Nineteenth Century:* Vol. I, *England in 1815*. London, 1949.

HAMMOND, J. L. and BARBARA. *The Skilled Labourer, 1760–1832*. London, 1920.

—. *The Town Labourer, 1760–1832*. London, 1917.

The History of The Times, 1921–1948. London, 1952.

HOBSBAWN, E. J. *The Age of Revolution, 1789–1848.* Cleveland, 1962.

HORN, DAVID BAYNE. *Great Britain and Europe in the Eighteenth Century.* Oxford, 1967.

HUNT, WILLIAM. *The History of England.* London, 1905.

HYDE, H. M. *The Rise of Castlereagh.* London, 1933.

JAMES, ROBERT RHODES. *Churchill: A Study in Failure, 1900–1939.* New York, 1970.

JEPHSON, HENRY. *The Platform, its rise and progress.* New York, 1892. 2 vols.

JOLL, JAMES, ed. *Britain and Europe – Pitt to Churchill, 1793–1940.* London, 1950.

KENNEDY, JOHN F. *Why England slept.* New York, 1940.

KLEINE-AHLBRANDT, W. LAIRD, *Appeasement of the Dictators. Crisis Diplomacy?* New York, 1970.

LAFORE, LAURENCE. *The End of Glory.* Philadelphia, 1970.

LAMMERS, DONALD N. *Explaining Munich: The Search for Motive in British Policy.* Stanford, 1966.

LAPRADE, WILLIAM T. *England and the French Revolution, 1789–1797.* Baltimore, 1910.

LECKY, WILLIAM E. H. *A History of England in the 18th century.* New York, 1890. 8 vols.

LEE, DWIGHT E., ed. *Munich. Blunder, Plot or Tragic Necessity?* Lexington, 1970.

LOEWENHEIM, FRANCIS L., ed. *Peace or Appeasement? Hitler, Chamberlain, and the Munich Crisis.* Boston, 1965.

LORD, WALTER F. *England and France in the Mediterranean, 1660–1830.* London, 1901.

MACAULAY, LORD. *Critical, Historical and Miscellaneous Essays.* Boston, 1860. 6 vols.

MACCOBY, SIMON. *English Radicalism, 1786–1832; from Paine to Cobbett.* London, 1955.

MAHAN, CAPTAIN A. T. *The Influence of Sea Power upon the French Revolution and Empire, 1793–1812.* Boston, 1892. 2 vols.

MANWARING, G. E. and BONAMY DOBREE. *The Floating Republic. An Account of the Mutinies at Spithead and the Nore in 1797.* New York, 1935.

MARSHALL, DOROTHY. *The Rise of George Canning.* London, 1938.

MATHIESON, WILLIAM L. *England in Transition, 1789–1832.* London, 1920.

MASSEY, WILLIAM. *A History of England during the Reign of George the Third.* London, 1855–1863. 4 vols.

MEDLICOTT, W. N. *British Foreign Policy since Versailles 1919–1963.* London, 1968.

MEHTA, VED. *Fly and the Fly-Bottle.* Boston, 1962.

MIDDLEMAS, KEITH. *Diplomacy of Illusion: The British Government and Germany, 1937–39.* London, 1972.

MINEKA, FRANCIS E. *The Dissidence of Dissent.* Chapel Hill, 1944.

MOWAT, R. B. *The diplomacy of Napoleon.* London, 1924.

The New Cambridge Modern History, Vol. IX. Cambridge, 1965.

NOGUÈRES, HENRI. *Munich, "Peace for Our Time."* New York, 1965.

NORTHEDGE, F. S. *The Troubled Giant: Great Britain among the Great Powers, 1916–1939.* New York, 1966.

O'GORMAN, F. *The Whig Party and the French Revolution.* New York, 1967.

OMAN, CAROLA. *Britain against Napoleon.* London, 1942.

PALMER, R. R. *The Age of the Democratic Revolution.* Princeton, 1964. 2 vols.

PARES, RICHARD. *The Historian's Business and Other Essays.* Oxford, 1961.

—. *King George III and the Politicians.* Oxford, 1953.

PETRIE, CHARLES. *The Four Georges.* London, 1935.

PLUMB, J. H. *England in the eighteenth century.* Penguin, 1950.

Portrait of a Golden Age, ed. by Brian Connell. Boston, 1958.

READ, DONALD. *Press and People, 1790–1850; Opinion in three English Cities.* London, 1961.

RICHARDSON, H. W. *Economic Recovery in Britain, 1932–1939.* London, 1967.

ROBBINS, KEITH. *Munich, 1938.* London, 1968.

RODGER, A. B. *The War of the Second Coalition, 1798–1801.* Oxford, 1964.

ROSE, J. HOLLAND. *Napoleonic Studies.* London, 1904.

ROSS, STEVEN T. *European Diplomatic History 1789–1815: France against Europe.* Garden City, 1969.

ROWSE, A. L. *Appeasement: a study in political decline, 1933–39.* New York, 1961.

SAVILLE, JOHN, ed. *Democracy and the Labour Movement.* London, 1954.

SETON-WATSON, R. W. *Britain in Europe, 1789–1914.* Cambridge, 1937.

SMART, WILLIAM. *Economic Annals of the Nineteenth Century, 1801–1820.* London, 1910.

SMITH, GOLDWIN. *Three English Statesmen.* London, 1867.

SOREL, ALBERT. *L'Europe et la révolution française*. Paris, 1885–1911. 9 vols.

TAYLOR, A. J. P. *English History, 1914–1945*. Oxford, 1965.

—. *The Trouble Makers: Dissent over Foreign Policy, 1792–1939*. Bloomington, 1958.

TAYLOR, G. R. STIRLING. *English Political Portraits of the Nineteenth Century*. Boston, 1929.

THOMPSON, E. P. *The Making of the English Working Class*. New York, 1966.

THOMPSON, LAURENCE. *The Greatest Treason*. New York, 1968.

THOMPSON, NEVILLE. *The Anti-Appeasers: Conservative Opposition to Appeasement in the 1930's*. Oxford, 1971.

THOMSON, DAVID. *England in the Twentieth Century*. Penguin, 1965.

THORNE, CHRISTOPHER. *The Approach of War, 1938–1939*. New York, 1968.

THORNTON, PERCY. *Foreign Secretaries of the Nineteenth Century*. London, 1881. 3 vols.

TREVELYAN, G. M. *History of England*. Garden City, 1954. 3 vols.

TURBERVILLE, A. S. *The House of Lords in the Age of Reform, 1784–1837*. London, 1958.

VEITH, GEORGE STEAD. *The Genesis of Parliamentary Reform*. London, 1913.

WARD, A. W. AND G. P. GOOCH, ed. *The Cambridge History of British Foreign Policy, 1783–1919*. Vol. I 1783–1815. Cambridge, 1939.

WATSON, J. STEVEN. *The Reign of George III, 1760–1815*. Oxford, 1960.

WATT, D. C. *Personalities and Policies. Studies in the Formulation of British Foreign Policy in the Twentieth Century*. South Bend, 1965.

WEARMOUTH, ROBERT F. *Methodism and the Common People of the Eighteenth Century*. London, 1945.

WILLCOX, WILLIAM B. *The Age of Aristocracy, 1688–1830*. Boston, 1966.

WILLIS, RICHARD EUGENE. *The Politics of Parliament, 1800–1806*. unpublished Ph.D. dissertation, Stanford University, 1968.

4. ARTICLES

ASPINALL, A., "The Canningite Party," *Transactions of the Royal Historical Society*, 4th series, XVII (1934), pp. 177–226.

BASSETT, R., "Telling the truth to the people: the myth of the Baldwin 'Confession'," *The Cambridge Journal*, II (November, 1948), pp. 84–95.

BEELEY, H., "A Project of Alliance with Russia in 1802," *The English Historical Review*, 49 (1934), pp. 497–502.

BOOTHBY, LORD, "The Baldwin I Knew," *The Sunday Telegraph*, July 16, 1967, p. 5.

BUTTERFIELD, H., "Charles James Fox and the Whig Opposition in 1792," *The Cambridge Historical Journal*, IX (No. 3, 1949), pp. 293–330.

CHALONER, W. H., "Dr. Joseph Priestley, John Wilkinson and the French Revolution, 1789–1802," *Transactions of the Royal Historical Society*, 5th series, VIII (1958), pp. 27–30.

[COBBETT, WILLIAM], "To the Rt. Hon. Henry Addington," *Cobbett's Weekly Political Register*, March 20, 1802, pp. 262–265.

—, "To the Rt. Hon. Lord Hawkesbury," *Cobbett's Weekly Political Register*, April 17, 1802, pp. 399–404.

COGHLAN, F., "Armaments, Economic Policy and Appeasement. Background to British Foreign Policy, 1931–1937," *History*, 57 (June, 1972), pp. 205–216.

COQUELLE, P., "Les Responsabilités de la Rupture de la Paix d'Amiens en 1803," *Revue d'histoire diplomatique*, XVI (1902), pp. 267–302.

DECHAMPS, JULES, "La rupture de la paix d'Amiens; comment elle fut préparée," *Revue des études napoléoniennes*, 44 (May–June, 1939), pp. 172–207.

FOX, EDWARD WHITING, "Munich and Peace for *Our* Time?," *The Virginia Quarterly Review*, 40 (Winter, 1964), pp. 41–58.

GARRATY, JOHN A., "The New Deal, National Socialism and the Great Depression," *American Historical Review*, 78 (October, 1973), pp. 907–944.

GILL, CONRAD, "The Relations between England and France in 1802," *The English Historical Review*, 24 (1909), pp. 61–78.

GODECHOT, JACQUES, "Le Directoire vu de Londres," *Annales Historiques de la Revolution française*, XXII (1950), pp. 1–27.

GROSE, CLYDE L., "England and Dunkirk," *American Historical Review*, 39 (October, 1933–July, 1934), pp. 1–27.

HUECKEL, GLENN, "War and the British Economy, 1793–1815," *Explorations in Economic History*, 10 (Summer, 1973), pp. 365–396.

"Ideology," *International Encyclopedia of the Social Sciences*, David L. Sills, ed. (1968), pp. 66–85.

INGRAM, EDWARD, "British Strategy and high command, 1783–1819," *Militärge-schichtliche Mitteilungen*, No. 2 (1972), pp. 165–172.

—, "The Defence of British India – I: The Invasion Scare of 1798," *Journal of Indian History*, 48 (1970), pp. 565–584.

—, "A Preview of the Great Game in Asia – III: The Origins of the British Expedition to Egypt in 1801," *Middle Eastern Studies*, 9 (October, 1973), pp. 296–314.

—, "A Preview of the Great Game in Asia – IV: British Agents in the Near East in the War of the Second Coalition, 1798–1801," *Middle Eastern Studies*, X (January, 1974), pp. 15–35.

JOHANNES, BARTHOLD, "Crisis 1936: the dilemma of British foreign policy," *Millennium*, II (Summer, 1973), pp. 3–16.

LAMMERS, DONALD, "Fascism, Communism and the Foreign Office, 1937–1939," *Journal of Contemporary History*, VI (1971), pp. 66–86.

—, "From Whitehall after Munich: The Foreign Office and the Future Course of British Policy," *Historical Journal*, XVI (December, 1973), pp. 831–856.

LANYI, GEORGE A., "The Problem of Appeasement," *World Politics*, XV (January, 1963), pp. 316–328.

LIPSCOMB, PATRICK C., "Party Politics, 1801–1802: George Canning and the Trinidad Question," *The Historical Journal*, XII (1969), pp. 442–466.

LOKKE, CARL LUDWIG, "Secret Negotiations to Maintain the Peace of Amiens," *American Historical Review*, 49 (October, 1943–July, 1944), pp. 55–64.

LOUIS, WM. ROGER, "Colonial Appeasement, 1936–1938," *Revue belge de philologie et d'histoire*, No. 4 (1971), pp. 1175–1191.

MACMILLAN, DAVID S., "Paul's 'Retributive Measures' of 1800 against Britain: the Final Turning-Point in British Commercial Attitudes Towards Russia," *Canadian-American Slavic Studies*, VII (Spring, 1973), pp. 68–77.

MURPHY, M. J., "Newspapers and Opinion in Cambridge, 1780–1850," *Transactions of the Cambridge Bibliographical Society*, VI (1972), pp. 35–55.

PALMER, R. R., "The World Revolution of the West," *Political Science Quarterly*, 69 (1954), pp. 1–14.

PHILIPPSON, MARTIN, "La paix d'Amiens et la politique générale de Napoleon I," *Revue historique*, 75 (1901), pp. 286–318; 76 (1901), pp. 48–78.

PRITCHARD, R. JOHN, "The Far East as an influence on the Chamberlain Government's Pre-war European Policies," *Millennium*, II (Winter, 1973), pp. 7–23.

ROSE, J. HOLLAND, "Burke, Windham, and Pitt," *The English Historical Review*, 28 (1913), pp. 86–105.

SCHMITT, BERNADOTTE E., "Munich," *Journal of Modern History*, 25 (June, 1953), pp. 166–180.

STEVENSON, J., "The London 'Crimp' Riots of 1794," *International Review of Social History* XV (1971), pp. 40–58.

THOMPSON, N. J., "The failure of Conservative Opposition to Appeasement in the 1930's," *Canadian Journal of History*, III (September, 1968), pp. 27–52.

TREVOR-ROPER, H. R., "The Dilemma of Munich is still with us," *The New York Times Magazine*, September 15, 1968, pp. 34–35, 72–84.

TURBERVILLE, A. S., "The Younger Pitt and the House of Lords," *History*, XXI (1937), pp. 350–358.

WATT, D. C., "Appeasement: the rise of a revisionist school?," *Political Quarterly*, 36 (1965), pp. 191–213.

—. "On Opposition from within the Elite: the case of Appeasement, 1933–1939," *Government and Opposition*, I (April, 1966), pp. 427–439.

WILLIAMS, J. E., "The British Standard of Living, 1750–1850," *The Economic History Review*, Second Series, XIX (December, 1966), pp. 581–589.

WILLIS, RICHARD E., "Fox, Grenville, and the Recovery of Opposition, 1801–1804," *Journal of British Studies*, XI (May, 1972), pp. 24–43.

WILLIS, RICHARD, "William Pitt's Resignation in 1801: Re-examination and Document," *Bulletin of the Institute of Historical Research*, 44 (November, 1971), pp. 239–257.

INDEX

E2